BUILDER OF BRIDGES
A BIOGRAPHY OF
Roy Hunter Short

T. OTTO NALL

THE UPPER ROOM
Nashville

BUILDER OF BRIDGES

A Biography of Roy Hunter Short

Copyright © 1980 by The Upper Room

All rights reserved.

No part of this book may be reproduced in any manner whatsoever without written permission of the publisher except in brief quotations embodied in critical articles or reviews. For information address The Upper Room, 1908 Grand Avenue, Nashville, Tennessee 37202.

Scripture quotations are from the King James version of the Bible, except where scripture has been paraphrased or otherwise noted.

The scripture quotations from the Revised Standard Version of the Bible (RSV), copyrighted 1946, 1952 and © 1971 by the Division of Christian Education, National Council of Churches of Christ in the United States of America, are used by permission.

Book design by Nancy Bozeman

First printing, March, 1980 (4)
Library of Congress Catalog Card Number: 80-50241
ISBN: 0-8358-0400-3

Printed in the United States of America

*D*edicated with great appreciation to all our colleagues, the Council of Bishops

CONTENTS

PREFACE _____ 11

MAYBE I HAVE BEEN CARRIED AWAY _____ 15

1 SUNDAY'S CHILD _____ 18

2 BOY PREACHER TO PULPIT MASTER _____ 27

3 SUPERVISION—TWO WAYS _____ 37

4 VIEWS FROM THE UPPER ROOM _____ 46

5 CALLED TO THE OFFICE OF BISHOP _____ 55

6 "BISHOPING" IN FLORIDA, TENNESSEE
AND KENTUCKY _____ 63

7 PRESIDING, PROMOTING AND PEOPLE-SERVING ___ 71

8 TRAVELING THE WORLD PARISH WITHOUT SADDLEBAGS ___ 79

9 CUBA AND CHANGES IN THE WORLD CHURCH ___ 89

10 BISHOPS ARE PEOPLE—ONE PEOPLE ___ 98

11 RACISM—PERSONAL AND INSTITUTIONAL ___ 107

12 SEXISM AND THE STATUS OF WOMEN ___ 115

13 ECUMENICITY—BEGINNING WITH US ___ 121

14 BISHOPS IN POLITICAL CRISES ___ 130

15 WALKING WITH THE GREAT AND NEAR GREAT ___ 138

16 DESEGREGATION—BY RECONCILIATION ___ 146

17 AREN'T WE ALL MINORITIES? ___ 155

CONTENTS

18 THE BISHOPS' CHANGING ROLE IN A CHANGING CHURCH _____ 163

19 THE BISHOPS AND THE COUNCILS _____ 171

20 USING, NOT ABUSING THE CHURCH PRESS _____ 180

21 FELLOWSHIPING WITH OTHER FAITHS _____ 188

22 METHODISM, UNITED, HAS A MESSAGE _____ 196

23 HONORING THE METHODIST HERITAGE _____ 210

24 "I HAVE BEEN YOUNG . . . NOW I AM OLD" _____ 217

Following page 112 there is a 16-page photo section showing the life and work of Roy Hunter Short.

PREFACE

John Ruskin once said, "The greatest thing a human soul ever does is to see something and then tell it in a plain way. Hundreds of people can talk for one who can think, but thousands can think for one who can see. To see clearly is poetry, prophecy and religion all in one."

Roy Short's life and religion are one and the same. And that life has been one of poetry and prophecy because of his unique gift to see and to tell plainly what he has seen. For this reason, the title given him by his biographer, "builder of bridges," is such an apt one.

It is with great joy that the editorial staff of *The Upper Room* has shared in this merited volume. Bishop Short was the second editor of *The Upper Room*. In fact, there is a sense in which *The Upper Room* was a sort of "bridge" to the episcopacy for him. What thrills us so is that Roy Short carried with him, into the episcopacy and into his ministry to all the areas of the church's life and into the far-flung corners of the world, that unique Christian flavor that is nurtured in a devotional life of vital piety—immersed in scripture and rooted in prayer, which is the essence of *The Upper Room*.

As the fifth editor of *The Upper Room,* I am humbled to be in the lineup with this great man, and I am challenged by the legacy of a worldwide ministry to which he contributed so significantly.

This book really came to be because friends of Bishop Short wanted his story to be preserved and told. Individuals from the Tennessee, Holston, Florida, Louisville and Kentucky Annual Conferences gave personal support to the production of the book by their contributions. The sponsoring committee included Mrs. William H. Criswell, Dr. Joseph W. Davis, Dr. Maxie Dunnam, Bishop Earl G. Hunt, Jr., Dr. D. Webster Johnston, Bishop Edward J. Pendergrass, Bishop Frank L. Robertson, Dr. Paul Shepherd, Dr. Orson P. Smith, Dr. Ben B. St. Clair, Dr. Albert W. Sweazy, Bishop Edward L. Tullis, Mrs. H. V. Weems, Mr. Gil Whittenberg, and Mrs. Frank Yost.

In a marvelously simple and sensitive way Bishop T. Otto Nall has told Bishop Short's story. I commend it with enthusiasm and appreciation.

MAXIE DUNNAM

The Upper Room
April 1, 1980

BUILDER
OF BRIDGES

A WORD OF EXPLANATION

MAYBE I HAVE BEEN CARRIED AWAY

*T*his is at once the easiest and yet the hardest writing task I have ever had. The easiest because Roy Hunter Short is, in many blessed ways, an ordinary minister who has become an extraordinary bishop. He has busied himself—and his family—at so many bishop's jobs, and done them with consummate ease—or, so it seems to an onlooker. His lengthy period as a bishop has proved again that, if a genuine believer in the Church falls in love with his or her job of work, whatever it is, there is no need for hobbies and extended refresher experiences.

Getting material has been easy, too. Bishop colleagues who wanted me to do the researching and writing assured me that Roy had files by the roomful. They have been helpful, especially the dozens of papers he has written on every subject that a bishop should put his mind on. But I have been given the task of telling the Roy Short story as it relates to the Council of Bishops. That has been easy, too, for he is a model team worker, and his ministry has been based on the corporateness—if you want to use such a mouth-filling monstrosity for such a soul-building idea—of the bishops. We are not penguins or puppets, but personalities, as you will discover by reading, especially the footnotes.

Much of the compiling has been done by interviews with the aid of a temperamental tape recorder. (Neither Roy nor I is mechanically minded!) Roy answers prying questions graciously and completely, even when he says, "You'd better check that." He has a prodigious memory and, best of all, an inexhaustible supply of stories, many of them included in the chapters that follow. Every one has a point, too, as you will find out. Like the stories in Roy's sermons, they are the windows that help us look into the preacher's transparent idealism, and when we have entered, we see the realistic world outside with new eyes and we hear it with unstopped ears.

"Paint him warts and all," some of the group whose idea this seems to be said to me, and this Cromwellian advice is always good, but what are you to do when your subject has no warts, not even a hickey or wen. That is where the hard part comes in—it is desperately tough to get Roy to say something bad about anything or anybody. He is too conscientious an historian to dig up dirt in the past, and too firm a believer in the firstness and lastness of God to get gloomy about the future. So far as the bishops are concerned, he is a strong and dependable link between the "no more" of the yesterdays and the "not yet" of tomorrows. If you remember how beautiful bridges are, with their tensile strength and their tremendous carrying power, you can call him a "bridge bishop" between the Old and the New. So, the news about this veteran bishop is good news.

Many of Roy's friends and admirers have been helping immeasurably with the writing and printing: Maxie Dunnam, Janice Grana and Charla Honea of The Upper Room, which is doing the publishing; Russell Q. Chilcote; Dr. M. C. Cleveland, our pastor in the First United Methodist Church, Clearwater, who has read the manuscript; and Mrs. James Love and Kathy Finkenbinder, who have puzzled out what Roy and I wrote to do the copying. Louise Short and Frances Nall have

MAYBE I HAVE BEEN CARRIED AWAY

read most of the chapters—and almost ruined what I had originally written on "Sexism and the Status of Women."

All of us, and many thousands more are glad that God, in his wisdom, sends Roy Short our way. And I, as an interpreting biographer, am glad to be "carried away."

T. OTTO NALL

Clearwater, Florida
December, 1979

1

SUNDAY'S CHILD

Roy Short's affection for Sunday began the day he was born—or before—and has grown into a burning passion for the Lord's day. He is Sunday's child, as the old nursery rhyme has it, with all the comeliness, wisdom, goodness and gaiety the jingle celebrates.[1]

Born on Sunday, October 19, 1902, baptized on Easter Sunday, 1903, ordained deacon and elder on September Sundays in 1923 and 1926, he was consecrated bishop on Sunday, July 4, 1948.

He came from humble parents for whom the day of rest and gladness was a blessed break in a hard workweek. His father, Jesse Peters Short, was a native of Willisburg, Kentucky. His educational advantages were few. He became a cook in the popular restaurant of Roy Hardesty, for whom Roy, first of the two Short sons, was named. Dr. J. Hunter Peak, devout Methodist whose name also appears in Roy's, was the attending physician. He was a boyhood friend of Roy's father. The Rev. D. L. Collie married Jesse Short and Minnie Badders, both 28 years old at the time, in 1900.

Roy's mother, the daughter of a cigar maker, attended the Louisville Girls High School and later clerked at the old John C. Lewis department store in downtown Louisville, and after that in the Sternaus store.

SUNDAY'S CHILD

METHODIST BORN, METHODIST BRED

The parents and their forebears as far back as Roy can remember were Methodist, and most of them attended Marcus Lindsey Church, Louisville, dating back to Civil War days. The church was the place where Jesse and Minnie met, and where Roy and Louise Baird were later to be united in marriage. Roy became one of the church's most distinguished pastors.[2]

Close by, in the old Eastern Cemetery, the venerable Methodist burying ground, are the remains of many Methodist figures, including Bishop Henry B. Bascom, who was elected chaplain of the Congress on nomination of Henry Clay.

Marcus Lindsey Church continued as a source of inspiration for Roy as he served other churches in Kentucky and three episcopal areas in the South. In a sense, all he did was a lengthening shadow of Marcus Lindsey raised to nationwide and worldwide proportions.

NOT ANCESTOR WORSHIP, BUT REVERENCE

"We owe them much, we can never cease to be grateful," is the way Roy and Louise Short speak of their own people. Roy remembers with special affection his paternal grandmother, Roxie Webb Short. She was born at Perryville (Kentucky, of course), and she was a teenager when her hometown became a Civil War battlefield. Her parental home was converted into an emergency hospital.

"She never forgot that harrowing experience," her bishop grandson comments. "She was a devout woman. She often told about hearing Dr. H. C. Morrison, Dr. John Wesley Hughes, Dr. L. L. Pickett (Bishop J. Waskom Pickett's father) and other leaders of the influential Holiness School of Thought. She had a gift for writing and frequently contributed to *The Pentecostal Herald* as well as the old *Central Methodist*."

Roy summarizes: "While the Holiness members of my family had some angularities—I had some trouble with the idea of the second blessing—they were good people. They were right in insisting that professing Christians ought to keep themselves unspoiled from the world."[3]

He tells of this humble and pious woman insisting that, like her Lord, she should be buried in a winding sheet—and this was so when she died in 1917. Far more important than what may seem to be a strange notion, she bequeathed to Roy and some others among her descendants a bit of the religious enthusiasm that made a lasting impression on succeeding generations of Methodists.

Roy's maternal grandfather, John Wesley Badders (nicknamed "Uncle Jack" by the whole community) was jovial by nature, and something of a practical joker. His father had died when John Wesley was only a child. His mother, Martha Utley, was a religious fanatic—or at least, her son thought so. For a time she left the Methodists and joined what was known as Maxwell's Holiness Band.

Roy notes that he never saw this grandfather in church except at times of family anniversaries, yet he was regarded as a good citizen. He was a Union Army veteran (Army of the Shenandoah), an active Republican, and occasionally delivered a spirited harangue from the back of a flag-draped ice wagon. A cigar maker by trade, he organized the first trade union of any sort in Louisville. He used to earn a little extra money by superintending the preparation of barbecues for political rallies. As a young man he had a brief stage career.

He kept a small shelf of important books that he had collected, and he gave the time and effort necessary to mastering them. He lived until his 80th year, 1924.

Roy's maternal grandmother was Josephine Gabriel Badders, whose father Charles was stricken with cholera on an Ohio River boat. The captain stopped and docked the craft, and the body was buried in an unmarked grave. Charles's widow, Elizabeth Timerlake Badders, later remarried, becoming the wife of William Wolfington. As a young woman she had a serious illness. It was actually thought that she had died and, as the custom was then, friends began preparing the body for burial. But there was a spark of life, and she was revived, although there was no cardiac-pulmonary resuscitation then. She was conscious throughout the experience, and lived for more than fifty years afterwards.

Roy's grandmother, Josephine Badders, devoted her entire married life to her family. She lived to be 80 years old, happy and radiant in spirit to the end. During her last twenty years she scarcely left her room, though she was not incapacitated. In her youth she liked to play the mandolin and dance.

BROTHERS: ROY AND STANLEY

"There were only two children in our family," Roy reports. "My brother Stanley was two years younger than I. We played together, slept together and shared the same growing-up influences and experiences. His adult work was with a well-known funeral home. He died in 1953."

Both sides of Roy's family lived their lives in the east end of Louisville, occupying modest rented houses in a largely German neighborhood. Grocery stores were on almost every street corner, fabulous bakeries that had attractions for growing boys and convenience shops of every kind. "An unhappy feature, there was a saloon on every corner or two."

Roy adds: "There was no particular pattern for the neighborhood. On the same block one would find several large houses with wide lawns and carriage houses behind, evidences of affluence; and alongside, the humble cottages that the working people called home. There were some black families in the same neighborhood. One of these lived next door to the place where I was born.

"A neighborly attitude prevailed. On long summer evenings the children played on the sidewalks in front of their houses, while fathers and mothers, uncles, aunts and cousins sat in front yards, trying to keep cool. It was an experience that helped me to identify with the mixes of classes and races around the world."

TO SUNDAY SCHOOL, TO PUBLIC SCHOOL

One of Roy's earliest recollections was visiting his grandmothers Badders and Short on the next block and going to Sunday school. He noted that each Sunday, the "scholars" (as they were called then) were each given a card with a brilliant Bible picture on one side and a brief review of the lesson on the other. He kept them carefully for the years 1906-1912.

His first teacher was Sue M. Davis, whose strong interests were temperance, missions and women's rights. She noted Roy's earnest face and keen mind. She took him to her home and to meetings across the city.

He entered school when he was six years old. It was the same Second Ward School his mother had attended, and some of the teachers who had taught her were still there when he came along. Boys and girls studied and played separately, but this was changed at the time Roy reached the seventh grade. He looks back:

"I remember the first day in Miss Bertha Steussey's class. She drew a circle on the blackboard and added a tail to the circle. She told us that this was the letter 'a.' None of the fancy ideas of today's education were known then. The teachers were all of the old school. Incidentally, I completed the eight years of training in seven years."

SUNDAY'S CHILD

One gets the impression from Roy that Sunday school meant more to him than day school.⁴ His mother was always there on Sunday and took her two sons. He joined Marcus Lindsey Church at the age of eight under the ministry of the greatly beloved George E. Foskett.

"After I had taken the church vows a hymn was sung by the congregation and all moved forward to shake my hand. They wanted to greet their new member, and some wanted to ask questions prompted by what the minister had said in the reception ceremony. Then he prayed that I 'would be numbered with God's people here and among his saints in glory everlasting.'

"In addition to attending church services and prayer meetings, I was present every Sunday afternoon at Junior League under the leadership of G. C. Wetstein, a local preacher whom all the children dearly loved. I do not recall missing church, Sunday school and Junior League except during the influenza epidemic in 1918, when schools and churches were closed."

An active boy, he attended classes and clubs, and the Boy Scout meetings at Wesley House. "The deaconesses seemed to take particular interest in me, and to be eager to help me grow. I guess I was given what we now call 'growth counselling.' "

COMING EARLY, STAYING LATE

In 1916 Roy started in the Louisville Boys High School. There was no coeducation on the high school level anywhere in Louisville. The faculty was a strong corps of men who had been with the school for a long time. In public the students always called a teacher "Professor."

With great delight Roy remembers Harrison D. Cannon, who taught Latin and encouraged his best students to join the

Latin Club. Roy continued his Latin training through high school as well as two years in college. He graduated at midyear and gave an oration on "Room at the Top," which won him a gold medal.

He became interested in Epworth League, with its motto, "All for Christ," which spoke to his all-out idealism. (In The Methodist Episcopal Church the motto was "Look Up-Lift Up.") He won various posts on the district and conference levels, and his speaking at many places led him toward the ministry.

After high school he worked six months in the old National Bank of Kentucky and in the office of a creosoting company. He says that these business experiences "sharpened interest in the temporal affairs of the church."

In September, 1920, he entered the University of Louisville. There he admired his teachers, as he always did, and worked hard, attending few students activities. One of them was the Poetry Club, and there two weeks before graduation he saw Louise Baird for the first time. He determined to try to meet her and get better acquainted.

Immediately he liked this bright, sparkling daughter of a hardworking ice cream manufacturer, but they were not married until Roy's second year in seminary. Their life together, founded on self-giving love and unswerving loyalty, was ideal—almost idyllic. Very much in love and long before they were married, he discovered Louise to be highly intelligent and a sturdy idealist, with a sensitivity and compassion that counted in every situation.

Furthermore, she has comic gifts that make it possible for her to laugh when it would be easier to cry.

When Roy was bishop and the Annual Conference was meeting at Bowling Green, Kentucky, she was riding in a car to a luncheon that was part of the Conference program. She was dressed up, wearing hat, gloves and a corsage given to her because she was to be the guest of honor.

There were repairs being made on the street and considerable confusion in the traffic patterns, with worrisome delays. At one point the flagman had trouble getting the lines of traffic through. The women complained that they would be late.

"I'll handle this," said Louise, and she opened the door and soon was standing beside the flagman. "I must hurry," she said. "There's a Conference luncheon and I am the guest of honor."

When the flagman tried to explain, "Now, Lady, I can't do anything," she seized his flag and directed traffic herself, soon getting the car through in which she had been riding. This she did, much to the amusement of the honking drivers, the sweating workmen and most of all the flagman himself.

She had found out what it meant to be a Sunday's child with Roy and joy!

BUILDER OF BRIDGES

NOTES—SHORT AND LONG

1. After describing the children of the other days of the week, the old nursery rhyme says:

> A child born on the Sabbath day
> Is fair and wise and good and gay.

2. The list of pastors included H. Q. Morrison (elected bishop in 1898) and Dr. E. W. Shor, who barely missed being elected in 1866.

3. The Holiness emphasis in Methodism, which flowered in America, centered in Wesleyan teaching on Christian perfection. It was a protest against the sterile religion of conforming middle-class respectability. Lace, jewelry and cosmetics came to church, where organs and even soft pews were becoming acceptable. Far more important, secular optimism was taking the place of a stern conviction of sin and experience of salvation. The Holiness people frowned when Christians lost their devotion to discipline. Roy remembers that it took him years to overcome a sense of guilt whenever he went to the movies.

4. A word about John Wesley's attitude toward Sunday observance may be apropos. He preached many sermons on days other than Sunday, and tried to take Holy Communion at least four times a week. He favored the development of Saturday and Sunday schools for boys and girls. Largely, it was the only day when they were free from the grinding toil of children in the first years of the industrial revolution. Sunday schools provided the only teaching many children had, and saved them from idleness and crime.

2

BOY PREACHER TO PULPIT MASTER

At 17 years of age, Roy Short preached his first sermon. He tackled a hard text from the Book of Revelation: "To him that overcometh will I give to eat of the tree of life" (Rev. 2:7). The date was a Sunday in August, 1920, and the place was Morton Memorial Church, Jeffersonville, Indiana, across the river from Louisville.

A few weeks later, in September, he boarded the interurban car in Louisville and bumped over to Orell, Kentucky, where members of the Kosmosdale Union Church met him and "carried" him (as Southerners used to say) to the church, where he preached both morning and evening. From that day forward preaching was always his favorite among the multiple tasks of the minister, and an important reason, no doubt, why he preferred Sunday to other days of the week.

He confesses: "Because I had only one sermon, I used an old Epworth League talk in the evening. And to my surprise, the people asked at Conference that I be appointed pastor for the charge that was to be formed with Kosmosdale as one point. Later, the superintendent confirmed the plan.

"I preached the first and third Sundays of each month at Kosmosdale, in the mornings and at night. On the second and fourth Sundays I was to be at Mill Creek.

"The pay was $30 a month at Kosmosdale where there were 30 members, and $40 a year at Mill Creek where there were eight on the roll, but 35 in the Sunday school. The Knob Creek Church was also on this newly formed charge, but most of the membership had moved away and the property had been included in the Camp Knox military reservation of World War I days. I preached there on fifth Sundays and raised $5.67 in pastor's salary for the year. It was a collection."

WALKING AND SINGING ALONG

In those days before marathon running became a civic sport, Roy thought it was a healthful practice—and the only economically possible way—to walk from church to church. As he walked, he sang in an attractive tenor voice the old camp-meeting air, "Footsteps of Jesus."[1] He trudged the circuits for three years. When he last counted, he had preached 6,580 times; the first three services back there in the summer of 1920 were the least advertised, but the most important of all his sermons, he later thought.

Soon after going to Kosmosdale he had his first funeral, and it was an experience that he will never forget, matching the experience of every minister reading these pages. His first wedding found him uniting, in the name of the church, Carl Robinson and Minnie Harvey. The young preacher was 18, and no member of the wedding party was of age.

The work on the circuits was hard, but the people were kind and understanding, taking pride in Roy's youth and forgiving his inexperience. His presiding elder (the change to "district superintendent" was to come during later years of his ministry) urged him to start the process of joining the Conference, so that he would have the security of at least a small charge.

The trip to Scottsville, Kentucky, and his first Conference

was made on what was called an "accommodation" train. It took the whole day and stopped at every station. He was quartered in a house three miles from town, sharing the bed with an elderly and highly nervous preacher—probably worrying about his appointment, Roy thought. He had his own concerns—not worries—because those applying for admission on trial had to take a series of examinations before committees.

The presiding officer of the Conference was Bishop Collins Denny—marvellous preacher, great parliamentarian and former schoolteacher. Roy held him in awe and admiration, partly because he had the demeanor of a teacher, to which he added, like most bishops of that day, the monarchal aspect of an authoritarian.

There were no minimum requirements for admission to the Louisville Conference then—certainly not the three questions that pioneers often asked beginners: "Have you had an experience? Can you tell about it? Have you got a horse?"

When the appointments were read out on Sunday afternoon—always that blessed day!—Roy Short was appointed to the Jefferson Circuit. It consisted of Mill Creek, which had paid $40 the year before, Fairmount down for $90, and Fern Creek, $50. Somehow the people managed to pay a total of $360; and the Conference added missionary funds. The circuit was too weak to continue, and it broke up at the end of the year with the individual churches being added to other charges.

In 1922, when Roy was becoming accustomed to circuit-riding by walking, he was appointed to the Mount Holly-Mill Creek charge, headed by a 200-member open country church. He had services at Mount Holly two Sundays a month, and the other two he served at the small Mill Creek Church. "I'll always be indebted to that strong group of young farmers and factory workers at Mount Holly," he recalls. "Mill Creek began to grow, and by 1926 it had 80 members. At the end of 1926, after four happy years with their undiscourageable young preacher, the charge was paying $1,250."

He had a model-T Ford to use in getting from his home and the seminary campus in Louisville to the charge for preaching and pastoral work. He found that the two ministerial chores go together like love and marriage.

"METHODISTS ARE THE MEETINGEST PEOPLE"

"I thought I was going around the world," Roy remembers of his trip in 1920 to St. Louis, Missouri, for his first churchwide Epworth League convention. In succeeding years it met at Nashville in 1921, Oklahoma City in 1922, Memphis in 1923, Dallas in 1924 and Richmond in 1925. He took the spiritual temperature of Southern youth and also met young personalities from other parts of the nation.

He visited storied Lake Junaluska, North Carolina, for the first time in 1923. Best of all, that year he attended the Student Volunteer Convention, where he sat and listened, prayed and cheered under the banner, "The Evangelization of the World in This Generation," a slogan that became a way of life for many thousands. The leadership of John R. Mott, Sherwood Eddy, Robert E. Speer, Robert Wilder and others was monumental.[2]

The evangelistic outreach of missions, both at home and abroad, appealed to Roy, a young idealist who had already been bruised and battered some by the world, but never conformed to it. The world vision and dedication of a Methodist layman like John R. Mott quickened Roy's mind and warmed his heart. He longed to see the "world parish" that John Wesley talked about and to serve, in the name of his Lord and his church, millions of seekers and believers in all nations, races and classes.

BOY PREACHER TO
PULPIT MASTER

GOING TO A PRESBYTERIAN SEMINARY

There were several reasons Roy picked Louisville Presbyterian Seminary for his ministerial training. It was at home, in Louisville. Then it had an ecumenical aspect to which he had been exposed at the Student Volunteer meeting. Besides, he hoped it would teach more than merely theology.

When he enrolled in 1924 he found a warm-hearted student body with some Methodists. The faculty he came to enjoy greatly: Charles Hemphill, who knew how to impart some of the knowledge he had about the second aorist and other Greek mysteries; Henry Dosker, who went beyond dates in church history; Jesse Cotton, who made Hebrew roots seem simple; and John Vander Muelden, who set some examples Roy is still following in homiletics. "I have used the basic principles of that homiletics class to model my preaching style for years." After he received his bachelor of divinity degree in 1927, he went two more years for the master of theology.

On September 1, 1926, Roy and Louise were married at Marcus Lindsey Church, Louisville, because her home church was under construction at the time.[3] Fifty years later, when the golden wedding anniversary came there were only five left of the wedding party of ten. In addition to the bride and groom, they were: Ed Cassell, best man; Bert Smith, a bridesmaid; Emme Lizzie Ratterman, who played the organ; and Florence Farmer, who sang. Dr. A. P. Lyon, who performed the ceremony, is gone; but Louise's father, 101 years old as this is written in 1980, and her mother, 94, were there.

NEWLYWEDS AT HOME

The next month the Shorts were settled in at the parsonage of Oakdale Church, Louisville. "We had a one-room church with an eight-room parsonage next door to the church," Louise remembers. "Four of the parsonage rooms were empty of furniture, and we lived in the other four."

The Oakdale congregation was a responsive and substantial one, numbering about four hundred persons. Almost all were connected with the Louisville and Nashville Railroad, working in shops, offices or on the road. Roy thinks back to the time when "the shops were only two blocks away and I passed by often at noon. I preached there, too. We had several engineers and conductors in the congregation. I have always felt close to working people around the world."

Hunter, the first Short son, was born on June 9, 1927. The whole congregation adopted him immediately and began to watch him grow. Louise took him to all the services. Everyone called him "Hunter Baird." It was at Oakdale that he began to walk and talk. "We remained there two years, and they were happy ones."[4]

BACK HOME AT MARCUS LINDSEY

In 1928 the unexpected happened, as it always does at Annual Conference—Roy and Louise were sent back to his home church. The membership was scattered over the whole city of Louisville. Roy admits: "I had been gone for eight years, and they did not receive me too cordially at first—or, at least, that was my impression—for they remembered me as simply a church member. But the attitude changed and I was accepted as one who had come back to help his own people.

"We had good congregations morning and night, and a prayer meeting that never dropped below a hundred. I preached on the streets in the summer evenings. Wesley House was a block away, and the social workers were active and helpful in the church. Louise and I had much informal

BOY PREACHER TO PULPIT MASTER

contact with Miss Ellen Gainey, the head resident, and members of her dedicated staff.

"Many of the old families we knew were living around the city, and they came back regularly on Sunday mornings. There was a noticeable gap between the older membership and the current membership of the church in the neighborhood. This put us into close contact with problems of the downtown urban church, and we never forgot the lessons we learned."

The next appointment, to Greenville, Kentucky, was a real boost at the start of the history-making depression. Roy and Louise sought to rise to the opportunity of ministering to the new people. Roy puts it this way:

"I found a marvellous congregation whose cultural level was unsurpassed in the Conference. The church building was only ten years old and the parsonage was the best in the Conference. Greenville was an intellectual challenge to me, and in many respects it matched or excelled what my seminary did for me."

Always appreciative of the laymen and laywomen in his churches, he had special commendation for those at Greenville.[5] "I talked to them in their offices and stores and on the town square. They would review my sermons for me and help me preach better."

Three months after the Shorts moved to Greenville their second son Murray was born. "He came to us in the Deaconess Hospital in Louisville, and we took him to Greenville on the Illinois Central's noon train. Our parsonage was on Main Street. The whole town made our two sons their own."[6]

All during the depression the Greenville church refused to lower the preacher's salary. This was largely due to two laymen who were top givers to the budget. "Clarence Martin was a happy, friendly man who ushered every Sunday morning and often dropped to sleep when I preached. He explained that he could trust me, without monitoring my every word. Charles W. Taylor was often a delegate to General Conference and was for years a leading layman in Louisville Conference affairs. He was a coal operator, as was Clarence Martin."

During the Shorts' last year in Greenville, Riley was born in the parsonage, since there was no hospital in Greenville. The congregation and the town welcomed the new baby with almost as much enthusiasm as that of his parents.[7]

At the end of the fifth year at Greenville, Bishop U. V. W. Darlington told Roy to expect a move. The bishop commented that, while all Greenville wanted their young preacher and his family back, "preachers are like trees—they take the direction of the wind, so I am going to put you in a new situation." And when the appointments were read—again on Sunday—Roy became superintendent of the Elizabethtown District.

BOY PREACHER TO
PULPIT MASTER

NOTES—SHORT AND LONG

1. Bishop Earl G. Hunt, Jr., says: "I doubt whether the bishop learned until his retirement that one member of his Holston cabinet insisted on humming the tune of 'Footsteps of Jesus' whenever the episcopal leader came into sight or stood up to speak."
2. Of course there were others in this galaxy of leaders who believed in youth. In 1948, when the aging John R. Mott was addressing the great company of youth at the Amsterdam Conference, he said: "Edinburgh, Oxford, Madras were ecumenical gatherings of those with few years left to serve. Amsterdam is an ecumenical experience for those with many years in which to go forth to accomplish God's high purposes. The hope of the ecumenical movement is the youth. You are more plastic and not afraid to make changes." (See also chapter 13, "Ecumenicity—Beginning with Us.")
3. Louise grew up in the Disciples Church, although many of her kinfolks were strong Methodists. She has often said, "I used to be a Christian until I married Roy."
4. Hunter Baird Short served in the Navy, attended the University of Mississippi and Vanderbilt University law school. He is married to Jean McElvey and they have three daughters—Nancy, Helen and Louise. He is a successful lawyer in Nashville, where the family attends West End United Methodist Church. Nancy, a Vanderbilt graduate, is a nurse at Childrens Hospital in Washington, D.C.
5. Roy says that C. W. Taylor was "one of the most generous men I ever knew and his wife 'a perfect lady.' " Among many others there was George Eaves, merchant; T. O. Hall, school principal; Charles Williams, druggist; Newton Belcher, blind lawyer.
6. Murray, the Short's second son, graduated from Emory University, joined the Air Force and served in Japan, took graduate work at Peabody College for Teachers and taught in

Nashville schools. For 15 years he has taught at Illinois State University in Normal. He is unmarried, attends First United Methodist Church, Normal.

7. Riley, third son in the Short triumvirate, served in the Naval Reserve, graduated at Vanderbilt and Candler School of Theology. He married Clare Malone. Sally, their older daughter, is a freshman at the University of Florida. Twin sons—Riley Philip, Jr., and Roy Hunter—are in high school at Leesburg. Susan is in grade school there. After serving churches in the Holston and Tennessee Conferences, the family moved to Florida, where Riley is a most successful pastor of Morrison Memorial Church, Leesburg.

3

SUPERVISION—TWO WAYS

The Church gave Roy two chances to check out the theory that the superintendency ("district" with Methodists, "conference" with Evangelical United Brethren) is the key spot in the Church's administrative system.

Although he had been secretary of the Louisville Conference, beginning in 1931 at the age of 29 and continuing for 17 years, he had no ambition to become involved in supervision or appointment making. He knew that stationing the preachers was at the heart of Methodist ecclesiology, but he never guessed that the Episcopal Message of the 1968 Southeastern Jurisdictional Conference would be pointing the finger at him when it said:

"The district superintendent has more or less always come under fire, largely because he directly represents the so-called 'power structure' of the Church. Quite naturally in a day like our own when power structures are commonly resented, he becomes a prime target. There are those who see the superintendency as an unnecessary and expensive office or an unwelcome promotional device, or an intrusion into the affairs of the local congregation. But those who think this, perhaps without realizing it, have moved towards congregationalism. The district superintendent, far from being a fifth wheel, is the very heart of the connectional system."

Roy's thinking at the time went this way:

"The district to which I was to be assigned paid only $2,400 the year before, when my salary at Greenville had been $3,200, fourth highest in the Conference. The district parsonage was old and in poor condition. Riley, our youngest son, was only seven months old, and traveling the district would leave Louise at home with three small children most of the time."

Elizabethtown and Lebanon were the district's only sizeable towns. Many of the small places, villages and open country locations were on mud roads. Starting at the top with the two best churches paying $2,000 and $1,800, there were five that offered about $1,200 and one more paid $1,000. All the others received less, about a tenth of the missionary salary in 1979. Roy reports:

"I was discouraged at first, but I got a grip on myself, for the district responded beautifully. I am convinced that it was going on this rural district that opened the way for a career of service for the general Church. I tried to identify with the people, who, after all, are my people. I held each year a district pastor's institute to help the preachers, most of whom were poorly trained. Also, I developed a small circulating library to supply their lack of books."[1]

The Shorts were not to be on a prevailingly rural district long, for in 1937, years before there was a six-year term for superintendents, they had dinner with Bishop Darlington one evening in Elizabethtown. He seemed to have some unexpected leisure the evening before Conference. Son Murray, who was then seven years old, said to him: "Bishop, please send us back to Greenville; and if you can't, send us to Louisville."

The gracious old man smiled kindly and said to Roy a day later, "I want you to come up to my room." Roy recalls how

SUPERVISION—TWO WAYS

it went: "It was an invitation without a definite time, and I did not respond. I was afraid he wanted to talk to me about placing a problem brother at Elizabethtown. But on Saturday night before the appointments were to be announced on Sunday, he told me, 'I want you to go to the Louisville District.' To this I replied: 'Bishop, do you remember what happened to Jesus at Nazareth? Louisville is Nazareth to me.' He answered: 'I will take that chance.'[2]

"Afterwards the bishop added: 'Do you know how many former presiding elders there are in the Louisville district? Thirteen!' He had this word of admonition: 'The Lord have mercy on your soul!' And the next day he read me out for one of the two plum appointments in the Conference—and I was only 35 years old."

COMING BACK TO NAZARETH

The Shorts moved into the Louisville district parsonage in September. Despite their youthfulness, the couple was welcomed by ministers and lay people. Obviously, everybody was eager to have the budding, young presiding elder make good.

The preachers were accustomed to having a Monday morning meeting in the old Methodist Temple. Roy changed it from a talkfest into a regularly programmed meeting on carefully chosen topics. With the help of E. C. Mayes of Broadway Church, the superintendent started a monthly district paper. And he made a strenuous effort to revive plans for church extension on a district basis. There had not been a new church in the Louisville district for twenty-five years. St. Matthews was the first to come under the new plan.

Roy calls to mind one method he used. "I took Hunter, Murray and Riley, plus a little niece, on Saturday afternoon and we distributed handbills over the area chosen for the new church. We began in a tent on Shelbyville Road and Frankfort Avenue on Sunday night. Meetings ran two weeks. John Lewis did the preaching. At the close of the meetings we organized with 34 members—my own father and mother, my brother Stanley and his wife Helen among them.

"Services were started in nearby St. Matthews Presbyterian Church, and were later moved to the Greathouse School. Dr. J. R. Savage, of the Kentucky Conference, was called from retirement to be the first pastor. He was living in nearby Crescent Hill."

EVANGELISM GETS TOP PRIORITY

On the Louisville district Roy had a chance to try out, on a district basis, several ideas about evangelism that had been buzzing around in his inventive mind. He was far from being an evangelism freak, but definitely a fan. He asked Dr. Harry Denman of the Board of Evangelism to come from Nashville and to direct an evangelistic campaign. He preached in every pulpit in the district. There were breakfast conferences with reports and suggestions (sometimes a testimony, too) every morning in the old Cortland Hotel.

With Methodist union in 1939, Trinity, Wesley, Market Street, Epworth and Grace, all former Methodist Episcopal churches, became churches of the Louisville District, and the Deaconess Hospital and Goodwill Industries, which had been Methodist Episcopal in background, became Roy's additional district responsibilities. In fact, the district office was located at the hospital. (Incidentally, the office was furnished by the widow of the Reverend T. A. Speckman, onetime Market Street pastor, to whose home Roy had delivered papers as a high schooler.)

According to the six-year rule, Roy was slated to leave the

SUPERVISION—TWO WAYS

superintendency and return to the pastorate in 1941, after his two years on the Elizabethtown district and four years on the Louisville district. The bishop postponed talking with him about a new appointment until the first day of the cabinet session immediately before Conference. Roy remembers:

"I had learned that Bishop Paul B. Kern [Nashville Area] had spoken to my bishop about the possibility of using me at McKendree Church, Nashville, and Bishop J. Lloyd Decell [Birmingham Area] had mentioned to him the possibility of my going to First Church, Montgomery.

" 'I want you to stay in this Conference,' the bishop said, but he had nothing to offer other than churches ranging from $1,000 to $2,500 less than the district salary. I told him that the salary differential could be worked out in our family council, but there was one Kentucky church where I did not want to go. My reason was that this church was on my Louisville district, and I knew that the congregation was divided over the pastor's return. The bishop said: 'Roy, don't name it!' With that the conversation ended.

"The rest of the week we worked on the other appointments. On Saturday afternoon he called me in and said, 'I want you to go to St. Paul.' I had to reply, 'That's the one church I meant.' 'I knew it,' he answered, 'but I'll work out a set of appointments that will take care of the man there and the situation.'

"When I walked out into the St. Paul pulpit the next Sunday I said nothing about being appointed there, but read my text and proceeded with my message. I tried always to go where I was sent, even as I expected my preachers to do."

ST. PAUL CHURCH IN WARTIME

The developing church to which the Shorts were sent was on the growing edge of the city, and it had a membership of 700. The first year the congregation raised the $2,000 difference between the superintendent's and pastor's salaries. There was a beautiful sanctuary except for the anticipated stained glass windows but they did not become a reality for some years to come. There was no educational building and therefore space for church school classes was at a premium.

In December of 1941 the Second World War began. The hope was that, under Roy's leadership, the church indebtedness could be paid, the membership built up to the 1,000 mark, and the foundations for an educational building laid. The first goal was reached, the second almost achieved, but the third had to wait for the next pastorates. The three-year stay of the Shorts bridged the wartime gap in the church's history, and it soon became known as the "cathedral church" of the Louisville Conference.

Roy continued to help his longtime friend Harry Denman with schools of evangelism in many places, ranging from Silver Lake, New York, to Lake Junaluska, in the South, and from Philadelphia in the East to Boise, Idaho, and Mount Hermon, California, on the West Coast.

CALLED TO THE UPPER ROOM

During a school of evangelism in Texas early in 1944, Roy had one of those dinner conferences that changed his life's journey, if not his life-style. Bishop Charles C. Selecman, who was president of the Board of Evangelism, wanted to have a meal with Roy and he brought along Harry Denman.

At the table the bishop began: "Grover C. Emmons is not well, and we want you to join the staff of the Board of Evangelism." Roy said: "I'll have to call my wife." Although he was sure what the reply would be, he was astonished to

SUPERVISION—TWO WAYS

receive a telegram which read: RUTH WON SIXTEEN LOVE LOUISE. He tells this story:

"I could not figure out who Ruth was, or why Louise would telegraph me that she had won some money. I remembered that it was racing time in Louisville. Finally, it occurred to me that she was referring to the wonderful words, where the Old Testament heroine was telling her mother-in-law Naomi, 'Whither thou goest, I will go; and where thou lodgest, I will lodge: thy people shall be my people, and thy God my God' (Ruth 1:16).

"Without my consent, the board's executive committee proceeded to elect me associate secretary. Although Bishop Selecman and Bishop Ralph S. Cushman urged me to accept, I told Bishop Darlington that I wanted to remain at St. Paul." In the spring of 1944 Dr. Emmons died.

When Roy arrived at Kansas City for the General Conference, he met Bishop Selecman on the street. The bishop said: "Roy, a few months back you turned us down. Now we are going to elect you editor of *The Upper Room* and this time I want you to accept." Hear Roy's comment:

"It was a hard decision to make—to leave the pastorate knowing that probably I would never again have a pulpit or people of my own. I counselled with Bishop William T. Watkins, then in charge of the Louisville Area, and he suggested that I accept, though he did not insist. He pointed out that Southern Methodism needed a number of leaders in key positions in the general church, and those of us in the South ought to take such opportunities when they came.

"I shall never forget my last Sunday at St. Paul. I kept saying to myself, 'You may never have a church again.' I baptized a baby and I could not keep back the tears when I said to myself, 'You may never baptize a baby again.' When I gave my last altar call in a church of my own, a man with whom I had been working for three years came forward, and another with whom I had been laboring since my pastorate at Oakdale fifteen years before. He wrote me afterwards, 'I went home and threw my bottle away.'

"It used to be my habit to preach from the left side of the pulpit, never behind it. Sometime after I left St. Paul the people there placed a small brass plate on the left side of the pulpit. It bore the simple legend: 'Bishop Roy H. Short preached here 1941-1944' and then there was added: 'Man does not live by bread alone.' "

SUPERVISION—TWO WAYS

NOTES—SHORT AND LONG

1. While Roy buried his early disappointments in identity with his people—and never lost his knack for walking, not grudgingly but willingly in their shoes—he often pointed out that the Church is never more or less than the people. In 1976, immediately before he retired, he wrote a paper on "The Appointive System."
He had four ways in which the bishop can use and not misuse or abuse the plan which vests the power to make appointments in the bishop: (1) He can decide that, so far as he himself is concerned, he will do all in his power to keep the appointive system what it was originally designed to be, a way to care for the Church. (2) He can decide that he will use the system to take care of all the churches. (3) He can decide that he will be the bishop of all the preachers—the weaker as well as the stronger, and the humble as well as the more self-assertive. (4) He can develop certain guidelines that he will follow and let it be known that he will follow them.
2. In the same paper referred to above, Roy paid his respects to those who claim much about the "autocracy" of bishops. He recounts what Bishop Darlington said about his last visit with Bishop Warren Candler, sometimes called one of the "old school autocrats." "The old bishop was in a particularly tender mood. He said: 'I hope I haven't done anybody wrong. I never meant to do anybody wrong.' " And Roy comments: "I have studied episcopal biography rather extensively, and my own opinion is that there have been very few times when the average bishop has knowingly done anybody wrong, and that the charge that a particular bishop is dictatorial stems more often than not from personal disappointment with some of the bishop's necessary decisions. Rather, it seems to me that the average bishop tends, much of the time, to be kinder to and easier on preachers than is sometimes warranted."

4

VIEWS FROM THE UPPER ROOM

*R*oy and Louise Short, with their sons Hunter, Murray and Riley, were more than a little homesick when they left Louisville, but they felt immediately at home in Nashville, self-styled Mecca of Methodism. They found themselves among such friendly Methodist neighbors as Donald M. Maynard, Wesley Carr, M. Leo Rippy, John O. Gross, Charles E. Schofield and Harvey Brown—all involved in the Christian Education program. The Board of Evangelism people, with whom the Shorts were to live and work, were equally congenial and supportive.

Roy's longtime friend Harry Denman had gathered about himself a dedicated and democratic company of saints-in-the-making. They could not match Harry in saintliness—and they never had the presumption to try—but in their way they, too, were on their way to perfection.[1]

On the board staff were Guy H. Black, the apostle of visitation evangelism; the inimitable Jim Chubb; and J. W. Golden, father of Bishop Charles Golden; with Editor George H. Jones, from Mississippi, who "kept store" while the others were roaming the world on evangelistic errands.

In the Upper Room group, which Roy was to head, there was Lucy Gray Kendall as editorial assistant. She had served in that capacity with Grover Emmons. "A remarkably gifted woman and gone now, the Upper Room continues to owe much to her," Roy says. Dr. Harry L. Williams, of the Central New York Conference, was business manager. Later he developed the Upper Room Radio Parish; and a layman, D. E. Jackson, succeeded him in the business position. During Roy's four years Harold L. Hermann came as circulation manager and Russell Q. Chilcote as editorial associate.

The newcomer from Louisville soon discovered that his editorship of this rapidly growing enterprise was to involve traveling and preaching as well as writing—perhaps more. He slept little the night before he made his first field appearance at the district superintendents' meeting in St. Louis. "I went by train and could hear the wheels clicking on the rails all through the night. They seemed to be saying to me, 'You can't go back, you can't go back.'

"I arrived at the Statler Hotel a distraught and disheartened preacher. When I ran into Dr. W. K. Anderson, son of Bishop William F. Anderson, he stopped me in the cafeteria line with the words, 'You and Manning Potts are the two biggest fools in the Methodist Church. For him to leave Greene Memorial Church, Roanoke [Virginia], to be director of the Crusade for Christ, and you to leave St. Paul Church, Louisville, for the Upper Room is simply unbelievable.' That was exactly the word I did not need at that particular moment."

Roy adds: "A few Sundays later there was a knock on our door in Nashville, and there was Bill Anderson. He said: 'I didn't help you much a short time ago in St. Louis, did I?' And I was soon to find that you get plenty of advice in the bureaucratic arm of the Church."

Like most other publications, religious and secular, *The Upper Room* received piles of miscellaneous mail in addition to the business letters. Roy had a plan: "I asked the mailing room to send this mixture of correspondence to me, and they would be my congregation-of-the-postbox. True enough, the members would be invisible to me, but hardly more invisible than my Sunday night congregations at St. Paul.

"Soon after arriving at Nashville, I began to receive a number of invitations to preach in various churches near at hand, and I welcomed them. By and by I began to realize that the invitations were coming from the friends of Harry Denman. I felt that he was a friend of mine because he was, first of all, a friend of God."[2]

Like every preacher who moves according to the itinerancy plan in the United Methodist Church, Roy had a hard time realizing that when you move, you leave one place and go to another. He had belonged to Bishop Darlington's Hundred Dollar Club, which supported a college "up home" in Kentucky. When no reminder for the $100 gift expected each year came to Nashville, he said to Louise, "You see, they have forgotten us already. They don't even ask us for money anymore."

He wrote to Bishop Watkins, who assured him that the college had been instructed to write all persons who had given in previous years. The president brought the matter to his secretary, who explained: "We followed the Conference report which said that Roy Short had gone to the upper room." Roy says: "She assumed that I had gone to the final upper room in the other world, and my name had been dropped."

EDITING IN THE WAR YEARS

The straitened circumstances of wartime brought problems of obtaining paper, mounting costs of all printed materials, added expenses of labor, distribution difficulties and assorted questions that only a publisher faces. But the circulation of *The Upper Room,* Dr. Emmons' brilliant answer to an old need, continued to climb.

A special packet was brought out for distribution among chaplains in the military. There was a khaki cover for the soldiers and Navy blue for the sailors. A German language edition was developed for prisoners of war, and this looked forward to the scores of languages in which this popular devotional guide would be printed, though as early as 1938 *The Upper Room* was being issued in four different language editions. To meet rising costs *The Upper Room,* beginning in 1948, became a bimonthly rather than a quarterly publication. Roy's editing proved again the value of specialized publications.

While Roy was editing he tried to find time to meet the opportunities for widespread writing about the values of the devotional life with its disciplines and holy habits. His articles appeared in papers other than Methodist. He did some writing for church school periodicals of several denominations in addition to our own innovative family of teaching materials and for *The Christian Advocate,* national and regional. And, of course, he wrote publications for the Tidings department of the General Board of Evangelism, with its growing list of valuable paperbacks.[3]

SEEKING QUALITY IN EVANGELISM

As editor of *The Upper Room* Roy was a working staff member, participating with his energetic friend Harry Denman in the development of policies. "It was expected that I would be a preaching editor," he testifies, "using my proclamation skills and experience in Annual Conferences, schools of evangelism, assemblies, and campgrounds as well as in individual churches." In his fourth year on the job he preached 361 times in the United States from ocean to ocean.

The Board sponsored a variety of different kinds of evangelism, for Harry Denman was a pragmatist who used any evangelistic method that would work. He brought in specialists who majored in their own methods of witnessing and winning. Roy's was to be pulpit evangelism. He wrote a small book on the subject that was widely used. He came with the fixed idea that much of what passed for evangelistic preaching was cheap, shoddy, and unworthy of the name, and he never changed his mind.[4]

He had a formula for what he called "quality evangelism." It had several recognizable characteristics.

First of all, he insisted that evangelism must be rooted in the truth. There has never been a revival of religion that has not found its basic purpose and motive in a rediscovery of religious truth. Quality evangelism must be true to the Bible, but not simply confined to the defense of the Bible (through proof texts and such). It must lift up the insights of the Bible for every person's life, convincing him or her of sin and pointing out the better way that God reveals. Biblical preaching calls to action on the assumption that the Bible message, properly presented, has its own convincing and convicting power.

Second, quality evangelism must be intellectually respectable. Even persons with nothing more than average school advantages demand intellectual integrity. Roy puts it pointedly: "I can think of nothing that is needed more in the Church than evangelists who are marked by intellectual respectability and strength."

Third, quality evangelism must be marked by good taste in message and methods. "It must refuse to exploit people. It must not use tricks to prompt a response. It cannot resort to financial appeals which result in a commercialization of the gospel."

Fourth, quality evangelism leads people into religious

experiences, both the first experience that we call "conversion" and those continuing experiences that we name "Christian action and growth." "The first experience need not follow a particular pattern. Some conversion experiences are sudden, some gradual. I recall imperfectly some lines of verse which convey an experience of gradual conversion":

> You asked me when I gave my heart to Christ, I do not know.
> There came a longing in my soul,
> I felt its flowers would fade and die;
> I longed for something that would satisfy.
> Then somehow I seemed to dare
> To lift my broken heart in prayer.
> I do not know, I cannot tell you when,
> I only know he is so dear since then.

Quality evangelism must be marked by a great love for souls, and a "tough" love for people.[5] Nothing surpasses the felt convictions of the evangelist for effect. The hortatory note must be strong. Evangelistic preaching asks for a verdict. In his books, pamphlets and tracts, John Wesley, a powerful evangelistic preacher, set us a good example.

Roy once made a talk to a group of church editors in Nashville on the subject "The Stewardship of the Press." Here he pointed out that those who write and print and distribute papers for Methodism must always help people who read, not seek to make money from their reading. "Our continuing purpose," he quoted, "must be the reforming of the continent and the spreading of scriptural holiness throughout this and every land."[6]

EVANGELISM: MANY-SIDED—GLOBAL, TOO

The worldwide outreach of *The Upper Room* taught Roy Short that evangelism must be at the heart of any real effort to change the world. He has little patience with what he calls "the cheaper forms of freeing people."

The Crusade for Christ and His Church, a churchwide program, grew out of the global consciousness stemming from the Second World War. The Crusade was more than a humanitarian desire to save millions from hunger, sickness, ignorance and other forms of human wretchedness caused by the destruction of war. Changing governments was the easy but always futile way of saving people from themselves.

Roy Short, as well as other Christian leaders, saw that changing hearts was the only effective plan for changing lives and achieving what Franklin D. Roosevelt called Four Freedoms—of speech, of religion, from want, from fear. But freedom to believe, to hope, to love—these reveal the positive side of all this. Roy liked to quote the familiar Bible truth, "Perfect love casts out fear" (1 John 4:18, RSV). And it was his understanding that we must be made perfect in love.

He made plans for family evangelism and promoted them through the Family Life Conference that *The Upper Room* initiated. Later Bishop Hazen G. Werner, who was elected bishop at the same time as Roy, popularized that family life movement and, through his tireless travels, made a worldwide impact on the varied problems of family living in many cultures. It offered a suggestion for the evangelization of whole nations, building on the family loyalty in Asia, Africa and other places where family ties are stronger than in Western cultures.

NOTES—SHORT AND LONG

1. There are dozens of stories of Harry Denman and his quest for Christian perfection, which he followed in his own unique way. He read few books except the Bible, though he produced pamphlets and tracts out of his own personal experience. A layman and a bachelor, he had no home, kept an extra change of clothing in his desk drawer at the office and often sat up all night on trains and busses. He usually ate Christmas dinner on a stool in the diner at some railroad station, and sometimes with inmates of a jail. He passed on the suits that were given to him to "those who needed them more." Often he was called the Methodist Saint Francis. One of the charming stories about him tells of the time when he was paying his bill at a restaurant. He chatted briefly with the cashier and concluded, in the way he usually ended his letters, with "Pray for me." She looked at him quizzically and said, "What have you been doing, Big Boy?"

2. Another Harry Denman story has him leading a group in prayer at a church meeting, and instead of saying "Amen" at the end, he said, "Sincerely Yours." One church editor wrote a biographical sketch of this hero of the faith and titled it "Sincerely Yours," for this summed up Harry's theology.

3. Roy Short's books on evangelism include: *You and Your Church* (Methodist Publishing House), *Spiritual Renewal for Our Day* (Tidings), *My Great Redeemer's Praise* (Tidings), *Evangelism through the Local Church* (Tidings), *Evangelistic Preaching* (Tidings).

4. Back then, Roy Short had the message that Bishop Roy Nichols proclaimed to the 1979 Congress on Evangelism at Pittsburgh: "The real enemy, we constantly challenge, is sin. Whether you explain it circumstantially, psychologically, environmentally, or 'originally' the immediate and ultimate consequence is the same."

5. With almost puritanical sternness, Roy opposed the romanticizing of love. He never thought that the biblical injunction to "love one another" meant fondling—hugging, kissing and casual "I love you's."
6. The reference is to John Wesley's counsel to George Shadford in sending him to America.

5
CALLED TO THE OFFICE OF BISHOP

*A*lthough the term "bishop" appears only twice in our scriptures—maybe four times, depending on interpretation—there are some sixty references in our *Book of Discipline*. We still use the lists of qualifications and duties in Timothy and Titus, but our elections are something else.

A number of United Methodists and Evangelical United Brethren, over the years, have refused to become "overseers" or "chief shepherds" because they thought themselves unfitted. Nine have declined consecration after they were elected, but five of them later accepted.[1] Nine have resigned.[2] Many others, for one reason or another, have withdrawn during the long, wearying process of balloting. But rare is the United Methodist who has not wondered what he, or she, would do if the call were clear and unmistakable.

What Roy and Louise Short were thinking on a July day in 1948, when they stood with a crowd near the stained glass window in Nashville's Union Station, is not known. But Dr. George Stoves, a retired minister, wishing Godspeed to the delegation going to the Southeastern Jurisdictional Conference at Columbia, South Carolina, was curious. He drew Roy aside and said: "They tell me that you may be elected bishop."

BUILDER OF BRIDGES

Roy replied: "I don't think so, Brother George. I may get a small shirttail of votes, but I don't expect to be elected."

Doctor Stoves persisted: "Don't let them take you out of the editorship and make you a bishop. Under our jurisdictional system bishops are too hemmed in. Look at Arthur Moore. What a great figure he was when he wasn't nailed down in Georgia. When Arthur was running, I said to him, 'I'm praying for you, Arthur.' And he said, 'Thank you.' And I said, 'I ain't praying what you think, Arthur.' He said, 'What are you praying, Brother George?' And I said, 'I'm praying you won't be elected.' Arthur wanted me to stop praying for him."

Jurisdictional Conferences have long had the practice of having a prayer before the ballots are collected by the tellers. There is no known case of a delegate wanting to change his ballot. But, one time, when the prayer was unintentionally omitted, a bishop was chosen on the 27th ballot, and the successful candidate was heard to remark, "It all goes to show what the Almighty can do when he isn't confused by too much advice."

How Roy Short and his Louise, who has exalted ideas of the spiritual opportunities of the bishop, plus their three growing boys, prayed during the election hours can only be guessed. Undoubtedly, that was a "dark night of the soul." But there is no doubt that, in retrospect, the most important praying had to do with Roy's private attempt to assess his own gifts and graces for the high office. Probably he faced such questions as these: Do I really want to be a bishop? Has my experience in the general work of the Church fitted me for the tasks of general superintendent in a church that is definitely connectional? Am I enough of a specialist in preaching to keep this central in a ministry that is essentially administrative, and enough of a generalist to make decisions for the benefit of the whole Church in the worldwide dimensions of a global

CALLED TO THE OFFICE OF BISHOP

parish? Am I willing to submit my future to the vagrancies of the democratic process? Can I suffer bruises of defeat without damage to my faith in people?

UPS AND DOWNS OF VOTING

Roy Short remembers the election as though it were yesterday:

"To my surprise, I led on the first four ballots. Then Marvin Franklin passed me and went on to be elected late Friday morning. This meant that the lines re-formed on the election of the second bishop. Those highest in the balloting were Dr. W. A. Smith, Dr. John Branscomb and myself. A seesaw situation developed with the Conference in great confusion on Friday evening.

"Dr. Branscomb withdrew his name, and Harry Denman suggested that I withdraw. I said to him: 'I did not put myself into this, and I am not going to take myself out; but if you want to, you can go back down the aisle and tell them to count me out.' This Dr. Denman proceeded to do and, when the Conference adjourned at a late hour, I went out with some friends for a dish of ice cream.

"When I got back to the hotel, some leading laymen of the Jurisdiction were waiting to see me. They told me to 'stay in there' and assured me that the Conference was determined to put me over in the morning. And that night I received telephone calls and notes from every Conference but three with the message, 'Stay in!'

"The next morning Bishop J. Ralph Magee, who was representing the Council of Bishops at our Jurisdictional Conference, asked me to walk with him downtown to the auditorium. He encouraged me in a tense hour. When the last vote of the evening before was reported, my total had dropped sharply because of the word that I wanted to follow the

Branscomb example and withdraw. But the first Saturday vote, when counted, showed a marked change. The voting continued and by noon I had the precise two-thirds required."[3]

THE END OF HOME LIFE?

"Louise was in the balcony when I was elected. In those days, in the South, it was not customary to bring to the platform the wives of newly elected bishops for recognition; and, because the Southeastern College of Bishops went into session, and I had to confer with them, it was late afternoon before I had a chance to talk with her after the election.

"When I returned to the hotel room I found her lying across the bed sobbing. Finally, she told me what she was thinking, and this was it, 'This will be the end of our home life.' I assured her that she need not fear."

The College of Bishops discussed where Bishops-elect Franklin and Short were to be assigned, although the decision would be made, of course, with the Committee on Episcopacy. The openings were in Mississippi and Florida. Some thought that Short should go to Mississippi and Franklin to Florida, and others that it should be the opposite way around.

The Alabama-West Florida Conference came to Roy and said: "We would like to give you and your wife a welcome dinner. May we ask her?" Let Roy describe the predicament:

"Cuba had been added to the new Jacksonville Area, and Bishop Purcell was concerned because he did not travel by air, and he would have difficulty visiting the Mission Conference in Cuba. Moreover, Alabama was his home (he had a marvellous way of pronouncing it 'Aalaabaamaa') and he loved it; and it loved him. So the Committee on Episcopacy changed its plan and assigned us to Jacksonville.

"The Alabama-West Florida Conference went forward

CALLED TO THE OFFICE OF BISHOP

with the plans for the dinner, and they derived much fun from entertaining the wrong bishop.

"I did not get to tell Louise about the change, and she was confused when someone said to her, 'You will be in Florida, but not in the Panhandle, our part of Florida.'

"I was scheduled to have the 4 o'clock devotional hour at the North Central Jurisdictional Conference in Indianapolis. After the consecration on Sunday we went to Asheville, [North Carolina], and I went on to my obligation in Indiana while Louise returned to Nashville."

THE STORY OF A TOWEL

"When we married in 1926 one of the gifts was a bath towel. It had a good deal of crochet work on it, and a big yellow flower basket in the middle. Louise said: 'We won't use this towel, but we'll keep it for the time when the bishop comes to see us.' (Only one visiting bishop came to our house, and Louise brought out the towel, but he didn't take a bath, so she put the towel away again.)

"It was hanging in our Nashville bathroom when I returned from Indianapolis. We never realized until later that we were keeping the bishop's towel for home consumption."

Of course, the beloved Board of Evangelism people had a magnificent farewell with dinner at famed old Maxwell House, later destroyed by fire. And the meal was almost as good, Roy admits, as in the days when his father was chef at the prestigious Pendannis Club, Louisville.

ROTATION OR LIFE EPISCOPACY

In 1967 Roy prepared for the bishops a paper that discussed the length of service of the bishop. It had these comments:

"A few sporadic attempts at the abandonment of life episcopacy have been made, the sharpest coming to focus during the depression years, but these attempts did not find strong support.

"At Methodist union in 1939 life episcopacy was retained, although one of the three uniting churches, the Methodist Protestant Church, did not have any form of episcopacy. Again, at the time of Evangelical United Brethren-Methodist union in 1968 life episcopacy was embodied in the Constitution of the Church, which represents that part of church structure regarded as so vital that it should not be changed except by a designated majority vote of the entire Church.

"Back of the concept of life episcopacy in United Methodism is the acknowledgement of the fact that the episcopacy is actually the cement that holds us together as a connectional Church. . . .

"General Conferences represent the whole church and write the law of the Church, but they do not hold the Church together. They are in session only quadrennially, and are composed largely of new delegates at each meeting, and when they adjourn, they adjourn *sine die.*

"The boards and agencies do not hold the Church together. Each of them is limited by its own designation of function and is committed to its own concerns. . . . The General Council on Ministries may be expected to provide some cohesion of program, but it, too, necessarily has limitations so far as holding the Church together is concerned.

"The episcopacy, however, in its continued functioning does serve to hold the Church together. [Francis] Asbury at first, with [Thomas] Coke away from these shores for 16 years, alone held the Church together between General Conferences by his constant traveling and untiring administration. Beginning in 1800 he and [Richard] Whatcoat, usually traveling in company, held the Church together; and beginning in 1808 he and [William] McKendree did the same thing. Since 1816 the episcopacy grew to the size of the present Council of Bishops but has continued to serve the same function of cementing the Church.

"In the episcopacy every smallest part of the Church and every individual member throughout the world finds continuing representation in its assigned bishop, and here every cause of the Church finds continuing advocacy. Any proposal promising to alter the essential functioning of so vital a body should be considered with the greatest diligence and care."

NOTES—SHORT AND LONG

1. An historical compilation made in 1978 by the secretary of the Council of Bishops lists these persons who resigned before consecration; and, though elected, never became bishops: Wilbur Fisk, James Roscoe Day, Franklin Nutting Parker and E. Stanley Jones. Five later accepted election: Joshua Soule, Henry Kumler, Jr., Jonathan Weaver, Atticus Green Haywood and James Kenneth Mathews.

2. Those who left the episcopacy of the denomination were: Leonidas L. Hamline, Milton Wright, William F. Heil, Frederick B. Fisher, George R. Grose, Chih Ping Wang, Frederico Jose Pagura, Raimundo Valenzuela and LeVerne D. Mercado. The last three are still living in 1980. Bishops Pagura and Valenzuela became bishops of autonomous churches; Bishop Mercado resigned because of ill health.

Of the 420 bishops elected by the Methodist and United Brethren Churches and predecessor denominations 111 were living as of January 1, 1980.

3. Bishop T. Otto Nall, reactivated after retirement to serve the Hong Kong-Taiwan Area, wrote an article published in *The Christian Advocate* for April 13, 1972, entitled, "A Bishop's Confession about Episcopal Elections." It contained this paragraph:

"It would save much anxiety and anguish and even anger (not to mention blighted careers) if aspirants, whether candidates or noncandidates, would make their peace with the fact that an episcopal election is neither a popularity poll nor a civil service examination. Necessarily, it is a political device (who was it said 'politics is the art of the possible'?) for choosing leadership and, therefore, a political event for which little preparation can be made. And now let me make this a genuine confession by citing my own election in July, 1960."

6

"BISHOPING" IN FLORIDA, TENNESSEE AND KENTUCKY

"*I* was determined to make mine a pastoral episcopacy," Roy Short remembers as he looks back to the fall of 1948 and riding the circuit that started with Jacksonville, took him to Miami, across the Everglades to Naples, up the West Coast to Tallahassee and back to the Jacksonville headquarters, with all the cities, towns and villages, orange groves and cattle country in between. "I must ride!" he said to himself, repeating the words of a Methodist worthy of pioneer days, but he decided to do the riding not on horseback but on what was known affectionately as an "iron horse."

"It was an overnight sleeper ride to Fort Lauderdale and Miami; a shorter railtrip across the state to Tampa and St. Petersburg and even closer to the state capital, Tallahassee. When I took the longer jaunts I could get a roomette, close the door and work with my books and papers in as much peace and quiet as one can expect on a train. Each such train ride was a long, undisturbed Sabbath for working."

He usually preached both Sunday morning and evening. "Years before I had formed the habit of writing out whatever I planned to say, whether in a sermon, an address or a brief talk. (Of course, I never took a manuscript into the pulpit.) My preachers may have felt that I did not come often enough, or stay as long as I ought, but at least I had done my homework, even though it was often done on wheels."[1]

In Florida the new bishop found the same problems with churches—large, small and middle-sized—that he had encountered as superintendent of the Elizabethtown and Louisville districts in Kentucky. Many of the older churches were struggling with fresh difficulties brought on by the population growth, with most newcomers from the North.[2]

New churches had to be built and old churches enlarged, especially in resort areas. Church extension was high on the priority list of Conference planners, and they welcomed a leader who had been close to the activities of the Board of Church Extension office, nationally centered in Louisville.

HOW INSTITUTIONS HELP

Roy found that the Florida Conference had close ties with the childrens home at Enterprise. The commitment was an enthusiastic one, but the bond with Florida Southern College was not so strong. President Ludd M. Spivey had taken over some years before when the school was on the verge of bankruptcy. An ingenious administrator, as well as a farsighted educator, he had developed at-large support from persons and foundations. One of his workable devices was to encourage support by naming honorary presidents, one each year. The Conference honored him for his remarkable talents, but left him largely on his own. Roy was eager for a stronger relationship between the Conference and the college. He found a way to link the educational needs on the campus with the church extension needs of the congregations, districts and the Conference itself.

The result was one of the healthiest church-college relationships in United Methodism. Roy was to find other examples of his belief that a Conference needs an institution, or several

"BISHOPING" IN FLORIDA, TENNESSEE AND KENTUCKY

of them, to prove its strength and build its morale. "An institution may become an instrument for the accomplishment of God's will," he says. "It is only when an institution is reduced to being nothing more than an institution which must be preserved that there is anything wrong about it—just as there is nothing wrong with personality as such, but there is something wrong when a personality becomes hopelessly ingrown and totally selfish."[3]

Vice-president Charles T. Thrift, Jr., for 10 years Dr. Spivey's helper, became his successor for another 20 years (one of the longest and most productive terms of service on record), and he gave sturdy educational substance to what a financial genius had begun. "Too long divided," as the Methodist fathers used to say, learning and piety grew together.

Property for a youth camp at Leesburg had been purchased shortly before the newly elected bishop came to his first Area. It was to become one of his favorite projects. During his second year the campus was dedicated, and he now delights to visit the new Life Enrichment Center. He has spoken often in the Youth Chapel beside Lake Hollingsworth.

Among the other institutions in Florida were the homes for the aging. They now number eight, of which only two—those in Miami and Lake Worth—existed when Roy was there. These were related to local congregations, not sponsored by the Conference. Jacksonville had a home for clergy and their families. Looking back to those momentous years, he remembers that two new districts were added—West Palm Beach and Sarasota.

FROM JACKSONVILLE TO NASHVILLE

Roy and Louise were saddened to leave Florida because they felt their work was not completed. They were always ready to go where needed. The 1952 Southeastern Jurisdictional Conference sent them to Nashville. The area included the Tennessee and Holston Conferences. The latter ran along a huge trough in the mountains, from Chattanooga, Tennessee, to Wytheville, Virginia. Bishop Paul Kern promised: "Roy, every bishop loves the Holston Conference." Roy had his own explanation:

"I could understand the enthusiasm of the Florida Conference, with many new people moving in. The Holston Conference, however, was an old Methodism, with much history; and yet it was marked by the same enthusiasm.

"The Tennessee Conference had been called 'the Jerusalem Conference' because Nashville was the capital of the old Church, South. The Conference lacked the vigor of Holston, but there was deep devotion and dedication among the people. True enough, the day had passed when the Tennessee Conference was the strongest in the Southern Church. The loss of Vanderbilt University had been a disillusioning experience for many Tennessee Conference Methodists."[4]

As an historian and undiscourageable friend of youth, Roy delighted in the progress of Emory and Henry College, oldest institution of higher learning in southwestern Virginia. It was named for Bishop John Emory and Patrick Henry. It may have been at the time in 1959, when he received the unusual degree of doctor of canon law, that Roy was particularly conscious of the Holston Conference cemetery, not far away and high on a hill back of the campus, and he wrote:

"One can walk along its quiet aisles and find there the graves of hundreds of the devoted Holston ministers and their wives, who wanted to be one in life and one forever." At any rate, there is not one of his many honors in which he takes more pride than that degree. ("Pride" may hardly be the word to use in connection with this Christian gentleman who has been noted for his gentle warmth, his unfailing sympathy,

"BISHOPING" IN FLORIDA, TENNESSEE AND KENTUCKY

his quiet gentleness, his patient courtesy and genuine humility.)[5]

Roy did not allow his affection, as bishop, for old and distinguished institutions to blind him to the needs of newer ones. He saw Tennessee Wesleyan, at Athens, lifted from junior college to senior college rating. He started a "Million for Martin College Drive" for the then small college at Pulaski, Tennessee. He thought it would do as much for the Conference to raise a million dollars as the money would do for the school benefited. Leadership in the campaign was taken by Mr. W. H. Criswell, long president of the Board of Trustees and an outstanding layman of the Tennessee Conference.

Largely under the leadership of Dr. Willard H. Blue, Roy saw the Tennessee Conference establish a retirement home called McKendree Manor, located near the famed Hermitage, home of Andrew Jackson. It became one of the best homes for the aging in United Methodism.

During Roy's administration the Holston Conference acquired the Oak Ridge Hospital, which did not become a financial burden. Asbury Acres, a home for retired persons, was opened at Maryville. Later the program expanded to include a home in the Virginia part of the Conference territory.

There was a strong Holston commitment to its institutions. Both the Methodist Episcopal Church and the Methodist Episcopal Church, South, had established schools and other institutions in this borderland, making a heavy institutional load.

BACK HOME IN LOUISVILLE

In 1964 the Shorts were assigned by the Jurisdictional Conference to the Louisville Area, the region of Methodism that they loved the most and to which they were most indebted. Looking out the front door of the episcopal residence in Louisville, Louise and Roy could see in the distance a water tower which was the site where they had their first half-date on a college hike. It was then out in the country. As Roy says, "Life thus came full round." He had not only been pastor of his home church, but superintendent of two districts and now bishop of his home Conference.

He turned the force of his abundant administrative gifts to the problems of his own people. As he had organized two districts in Florida and one in Holston, he formed Conference councils in both Louisville and Kentucky, anticipating the general church model which came in 1968.

The facilities of Camp Loucon, the Louisville Conference youth camp, were greatly expanded, as was the summer program. The Kentucky Mountain mission, a project representing the application of the Goodwill Industries pattern to a mountain situation, and sponsored by the Kentucky Conference, was extended and enriched in those days.

Continuing support was given to five hospitals—Methodist Evangelical at Louisville, Henderson, Good Samaritan at Lexington, Pikeville and Red Bird Mission. Three colleges were helped: Kentucky Wesleyan, Union and Lindsay Wilson. The childrens home at Versailles and a home for the aging at Louisville and six Wesley Foundations were beneficiaries of careful leadership.

An important development during the Short administration was the mergers involving former Evangelical United Brethren churches. There were three in Louisville, one in Newport across the Ohio river from Cincinnati (and the only Evangelical United Brethren Church within the borders of the Kentucky Conference) and one in Cloverport which had been related to Evangelical United Brethren work in Indiana. There were also several rural churches in the Campbellsville District. When the Evangelical United Brethren joined with

"BISHOPING" IN FLORIDA, TENNESSEE AND KENTUCKY

the Methodists in 1968 they brought into the Louisville Area the Red Bird Mission, the most significant home mission work in all Appalachia.

WHAT IS A PASTORAL BISHOP?

Roy never permitted his administrative work to interfere with his preaching, and, likewise, he did not allow his preaching to eclipse his pastoring. *Pastoring* is the word to describe what Roy did.

"I always thought of the episcopacy as a pastoral episcopacy," he says. "I let it be known that my office door was always open, and any person, clergy or lay, was free to drop in at any time, without appointment. I did not find this relaxed pattern too burdensome. I kept office hours, but did not have too rigid a schedule. And, although I was busy with many meetings and my share of overseas travel (and the secretaryship of the Council of Bishops) I tried always to be available to talk with those who needed to see me."

How he managed this will be detailed in the next chapter.

NOTES—SHORT AND LONG

1. The St. Johns River Conference of the Methodist Episcopal Church, which dated back to 1887, was joined with the Florida Conference of the Methodist Episcopal Church, South in 1939 at Unification. The Conference was part of the Atlanta Area, which the Jurisdictional Conference deemed too large, and insisted that the new Area be located in Florida. Under Bishop Short's and Bishop John W. Branscomb's presidencies the headquarters was at Jacksonville, but Bishop James Henley moved it to Lakeland.

2. A venerable joke concerns an old man (Florida cracker) who was asked what Floridians lived on. He said: "Yams in the summer time and you'uns in the winter time."

3. The quotation is from Bishop Short's paper on "The Church as Institution and Instrument." He maintained that local churches can be institutions without the curse of institutionalism. For one quadrennium he was head of the plans to strengthen the local church, especially the smaller churches. He became known as "Bishop of the Small Churches."

4. Two Short sons and several grandchildren hold degrees from Vanderbilt.

5. The list cited is from Bishop Earl G. Hunt, Jr.'s tribute on the occasion of Bishop Short's retirement in June 1972. The sermon was preached at the Louisville Annual Conference session in St. Paul Church, June 26.

7

PRESIDING, PROMOTING AND PEOPLE-SERVING

*S*oon after he joined the episcopal ranks Roy Short discovered that not the least important of a bishop's functions is people-watching, with the purpose of people-serving. For the authentic minister, persons always win in the age-old rivalry between people and books, although Roy has thought enough of books to write some that had considerable circulation. And he has found that the most significant—and loveable—persons are not always those who have the big names.

For example, there was Brother What's-His-Name[1] who actually spent much of his Conference time in the churchyard swapping stories and talk with the brethren. Hear Roy's account:

"We were in the midst of a spirited debate, with Bishop Darlington presiding. The hero of our story was outside listening with one ear to the loudspeaker—only one ear, mind you, for that was the first time we had such gadgets at Conference. He said, 'I think I'll go in there and make a speech.' When he walked down the aisle and asked for the floor, the bishop said to him, 'Which side are you on?' And the man from the churchyard bleachers said, 'Which side is up next?' The bishop answered, 'The negative,' and he replied, 'I'll speak on that'; and he did."

BUILDER OF BRIDGES

Roy believes in the rules of parliamentary procedure, but in presiding he assumed that preachers and lay people at Annual Conference came for a spiritual experience.[2] "I tried to avoid what was merely a business meeting. I planned for much preaching and a variety of worship experiences. I found a place for humor, and occasionally I started a song that I thought pertinent to what we were doing.

"Furthermore, I tried to recognize the presence of those who were usually overlooked at Conference. I remember that once, in the Florida Conference session, I sent a note to one of the pastors who were serving as what was called 'glade preachers.' He had spent all his ministry in the hard places. My note asked that he come to the platform. I am sure that he thought this might have something to do with his appointment. He was clearly worried. I said simply, 'At the close of the session I want you to have the benediction.' (He stood there with tears in his eyes when he had done what I asked.) 'Will it be in the minutes that I had the benediction?' he asked. 'Certainly it will be,' was my answer. And he commented: 'That will be the first time my name has been in the minutes except for the roll call.' He added: 'I tried to do my best.'"

Roy, who is known as an extraordinarily competent presiding officer has some simple rules for presiding, whether it is in a committee meeting, a sizeable board, an Annual Conference or the General Conference. He says:

"Stay out where everybody can see you. Look in different directions from time to time so that no section of the body feels neglected. If it's the General Conference, don't pay attention to notes asking for the floor, even if sent up by a fellow bishop wanting the floor for a friend. Keep the motion under discussion clearly before the body. Never ask: 'Does anyone else have anything to say?' Respect the rights of the majority to make decisions, but also the right of the minority to be heard fully before the vote is taken. Also the right of individual members to discuss the issue."[3]

Roy recognizes the fact that some gifted and truly great bishops have not been good presiding officers. Bishop Hubbard Hinde Kavanaugh used to go to sleep in the chair sometimes. Bishop O. P. Fitzgerald was not suited to presiding and often, when a parliamentary situation became confused, he would ask the Conference to sing a hymn. Bishop William Fraser McDowell was no parliamentarian; he often asked Bishop E. G. Andrews to sit beside him saying, "I will occupy the chair but Andrews will preside."

Roy admires unfailing courtesy. He remembers how Bishop Willis J. King would say, when a brother asked a question after debate was no longer in order, "My brother, there is a thin line between asking a question and making an argument, and I think you have stepped over that line."

APPOINTMENTS AND DISAPPOINTMENTS

Admitting that the appointive system has always been subject to certain strains because the connectional ministry is an interrelated ministry, Roy is convinced that the problem is more "discipline" than "system." Bishop A. Frank Smith used to say that one of the necessary but sad features of the itinerancy is that it has so much in common with a horse race. All the horses start out together, but after a bit the better horses pull out ahead. Roy tells the story and adds:

"Some preachers will never understand why some things happen to other preachers and not to themselves. And to make matters worse, too many of the brethren who do see their dreams come true are seemingly so elated over what has happened to them that they seem totally unaware of the possible effect on others. Not too many are like John G. Whittier's little maid who said to her small boy friend in the spelling match":

> "I'm sorry that I spelt the word;
> I hate to go above you,
> Because"—the brown eyes lower fell—
> "Because, you see, I love you!"

Roy did a paper for the bishops in which he developed some guidelines for appointment making by episcopal leaders and their cabinets. He wrote of the spirit of the age and said:

"The older Methodist preacher who used to boast that he had never refused an appointment seems to be largely passing, and a more self-assertive preacher seems to be emerging. I do not recall having heard myself the word 'promotion' used in a cabinet session during my years as a superintendent 40 years ago—and I never heard the terrible word 'demotion' and, worse still, 'demote' until I went to Nashville in 1952."

Before the 1976 General Conference Roy dealt, frankly and quite fully, with some efforts to limit still further the power of the bishops and cabinets. He felt that much could be done to guarantee fairness in appointment making, staying within the framework of existing legislation, and he had these suggestions:

"The bishop can refuse to allow the appointive system to be reduced to something compatible to the protection of a labor union. He can insist on giving the same consideration and attention to the smaller appointments as that given to the larger ones. He can hear every church and every preacher who desires to talk with him. He can involve the whole cabinet in making every appointment."

Roy concludes: "From time to time the bishop will need to take a firm position and sometimes even to be severe in dealing with demanding preachers, long entrenched preachers,

PRESIDING, PROMOTING AND PEOPLE-SERVING

and ineffective preachers—and with churches making unreasonable requests."

APPOINTING DISTRICT SUPERINTENDENTS

"In the matter of appointing district superintendents, I tried to keep a balanced cabinet. In all groups there are different schools of thought. I tried, therefore, to have my advisers representative of differing viewpoints in the Conference, and I tried to remember that I was the bishop of all.

"Ministerial supply was our most bothersome problem," Roy recalls as he looks back to the days when it was a struggle to keep the churches supplied with good ministers. "We tried to get trained persons, and to keep them as long as we could." Hear him further:

"In our part of the Church in former years, most of the appointments were made at the seat of the Conference. Cabinet meetings came after the sessions and often ran far into the night. Sometimes the bishop would have to summon someone to preside while he went out and met with his cabinet in special session. The appointments were often total surprises. As the Conference proceeded there was naturally a mounting pressure, and sometimes the steam climbed high.

"I felt I could not hold the Conference and have cabinet meetings at the same time. I formed the habit of going, some while before Conference, into the districts for consultation with groups and persons who wanted to talk with me. I always had the district superintendent with me when I visited his district, and he was present at the interviews. When the cabinet met I had this firsthand knowledge of each situation. Our pre-Conference cabinet meetings were held elsewhere than at the seat of the Conference.

"I would ask each cabinet member to bring his wife to such meetings so that, after the cabinet adjourned, they would be returning to a family situation and not sit up half the night with some other superintendent trying to figure ways of outmaneuvering other superintendents. Of course, I did not hesitate to move superintendents from one district to another if there was reason for doing so. I discouraged each superintendent from thinking that his own district was a little principality.

"In making the appointments I kept the lead myself, but I involved the whole cabinet in the consideration of every appointment. I asked for nominations for every appointment, large or small, allowing each superintendent to make nominations, if he desired, whether the charge under consideration was in his district or not."

DESIGNING THE CONFERENCE SCHEDULE

"In working out the Conference program I tried to avoid a tight schedule, preferring to keep it flexible, so that nobody knew what would be called next. We had little problem with finding half the membership outside on the street or in the bookroom gossiping while we were in session.[4]

"Every Sunday, so far as possible, I went into the churches, asking the superintendents to work out my schedule. My practice was to allow a few Sundays to each superintendent, saying, 'Use me in your district wherever you think I can do the most good.' This avoided giving too much of my time to the stronger or more demanding churches. In my twenty-four years as a general superintendent I never went into a district without the district superintendent being with me.

"Louise and I followed the pattern of asking the wives to come with the cabinet members whenever we met for a retreat. Each fall we went to a Conference center or state park. We carried all the expenses ourselves. We spent the time talking about goals and plans and methods to be followed in the Conference program. There was also Bible study, and we left periods for discussion of basic issues in the life of the Church. Having the spouses as part of the group did much for the development of cabinet morale.

"At the end of our twelve years in the Nashville Area we had all men who had served on the cabinet during our three quadrenniums, and also our wives and also the widows of former cabinet members, with us for a beautiful occasion."

WHAT ABOUT A MOBILE EPISCOPACY?

On the basis of twenty-four years Roy says, unless a bishop is elected for a short term, he ought to move at least once, for his own good and the good of the Church. He says: "We cannot logically ask ministers to move unless we are willing to move ourselves. If a bishop is effective, I think more than one Area should have the advantage of his effectiveness. If he is not too effective, I think other Areas should take their turn with him—for they probably helped elect him.

"Furthermore, I believe that only a mobile episcopacy is truly a general superintendency, as Methodism has always considered its episcopacy to be. There has always been some sentiment in the Church for a term episcopacy, but United Methodists have again and again come down in favor of life episcopacy. We have thought of our episcopacy as fully mobile, avoiding the resemblance of a diocesan episcopacy."

Still this means, of course, that the gifts and graces to give real pastoral care are expected of all bishops, and they must do conscientious people-serving.

NOTES—SHORT AND LONG

1. The pastor was Rev. P. L. King at a Louisville Conference meeting at Elizabethtown, Kentucky.
2. At a briefing session for bishops who might be asked to preside at the 1980 General Conference, Bishop Paul Milhouse presented a paper that included an interesting fact about General Henry Martyn Roberts, and his famed "Rules of Order." Roberts developed them after he had an unpleasant time presiding at a town meeting in a Baptist church at New Bedford, Massachusetts.
3. Bishop Jack M. Tuell quotes a letter from Bishop Nolan B. Harmon on presiding: "Some bishops act as though the body is a social meeting, anxious to be polite, and afraid of being thought not fair to all. The best presiders see the body for what it is, and relentlessly put motions and drive ahead. The bishop who waits and asks if 'anything else is to be said,' or hesitates to put the question, will find twenty persons leaping at him to take the floor. . . . Conferences appreciate a strict presider. When they feel they have got an uncertain one—and they sense this immediately—then they begin to go to pieces."
4. Roy Short has an enviable record for attending Council of Bishops meetings. He never missed one in 32 years, up to the 1980 General Conference. And he has seldom been out of the room at any session.

8

TRAVELING THE WORLD PARISH WITHOUT SADDLEBAGS

*Y*ears after Bishop Urban Valentine Williams Darlington was Roy's bishop in Kentucky, Roy made a pilgrimage to the Darlington home at Huntington, West Virginia. Let Roy tell what they saw:

"In the bishop's study everything was precisely as he had left it years before. The books were on the shelves, writing and other articles on the desk, his old battered typewriter beside his armchair, but what impressed me most was the coat and the hat hanging on the peg behind the door where he always kept them, ready to go on one more journey for the Church and the Lord he loved.

"Many memories crowded in. One of them brought me back to 1935. At Conference in Henderson [Kentucky], early one morning, he asked me to drive him out to a park on the edge of town. Upon reaching the place he suggested that we pull over to the side of the road. He looked at me and said: 'Roy, you grew up in town, and I guess you don't know much about trees.' I replied that I didn't. He said: 'If you had grown up in the country you would know that the trees take the direction of the wind, and young preachers do the same thing. You have been at Greenville five years, and they want you back, but I don't want you to take the direction of the wind.'

"I replied: 'Well, Bishop, the *Discipline* says that's what you can do' [not let him take the direction of the wind]. He never got specific about where I would go, but at the end of the week, to my surprise, he read me out for a country district. I was only 32 years old, and now I was what the Church called a 'presiding elder.'

"I thought of Bishop Darlington as a typical old-fashioned Southern bishop. He traveled abroad as he did at home, identifying himself with the people, learning their needs and ministering to them. For years (1926 to 1934) he served the Southern Church's new European Area, including Belgium, Poland and Czechoslovakia. Later, he was called back from retirement to administer in Mississippi for three years.

"He taught me to keep my spiritual saddlebags packed, and my coat and hat on the peg behind the door."

BELIEVING IN THE ITINERANCY

The ministry that we know has always been an itinerant ministry, or a "traveling connection," if you will. An aged or infirm preacher who was no longer able to endure the rigors of travel formerly was not "retired" but "released from the obligation to travel." Today, the retired minister is not exempted from any other obligation taken with the ordination or consecration vows except the promise to travel.[1]

Since Louise Short is not only a tireless traveler but also a sharp observer ("She has to see the other side of every hill," Roy says), she has accompanied him on most of his episcopal visits and has helped immeasurably in reporting to the other bishops and their wives and the whole Church.

For some twenty years the Council has sent its members on official trips overseas from the United States.[2] Roy considers the journeys he has made on these two-month, in-depth studies among the most rewarding in his experience. He has

TRAVELING THE WORLD PARISH
WITHOUT SADDLEBAGS

traveled the world parish, and he views with some alarm any trend towards making our Methodism "an American church with worldwide appendages."[3]

BEGINNING WITH BRAZIL AND PERU

The first visitation was to Peru and Brazil, near neighbors to people whose homes in the United States have a Southern exposure. Roy chose Latin America because he had been assigned the work in Cuba along with the whole state of Florida, except for the Panhandle. The Shorts went from Miami to Lima, where they were guests of Bishop Enrique Carlos Balloch, who showed them the high school in Lima, some of the typical churches, large and small, and a shantytown, where a missionary was experimenting with the new idea of living with the people.

In Brazil, Bishop César F. Dacorso, first native bishop among Brazilian Methodists, welcomed the Shorts. The work there had been sponsored by the Methodist Episcopal Church, South, and was a highly favored mission field. Bishop John M. Moore, in particular, made a remarkable record there (1918-22) during his first quadrennium as bishop.

One morning Roy and Louise attended a retreat that began at 6 o'clock and it continued with such rapt attention that nobody paid any heed when breakfast was placed on the table. The prayers and testimonies went on as the breakfast was removed, and the meeting did not adjourn until noon. The same startling pattern was followed at coffee time. That retreat was led by the saintly Bishop Cyrus Dawsey, who retired in Florida.

"I could not understand a word that was spoken," Roy recalls, "but I remember few times in my life when I was more conscious of spiritual power." The Shorts also attended a joint meeting with Baptist missionaries, and were glad to see

Methodists and Baptists working so well together. All this happened in Rio de Janeiro.

On a later trip to Brazil, which Roy made for the Council of Bishops to the autonomous Methodist Church, he hoped that he would be able to ease tensions that had developed. This was in 1969, and he found a much different spirit from that of a dozen years back. The seminary was closed and some other schools were suspended. There was ill-feeling between some of the institutions and their episcopal leaders, and actually some friction between the bishops themselves.

At the Annual Conference in Rio de Janeiro, Roy discovered that the resident bishop, who had not joined in the invitation for him to come, and who was religiously and economically conservative, was at odds with some of the others. "He was not antagonistic, but he did not open up until Louise paid some special attention to his little granddaughter. Then he was friendly." Roy explains:

"I do not know how much of this tension was due to leftist movements in the churches, and how much to ecclesiastical politics. Perhaps the differences were somewhat like those we had in our own country when one compares the way we were living in the fifties and early sixties with our life-styles in the late sixties and seventies." Roy adds:

"I think that our bishops in Brazil and those we saw in Argentina and Chile, when we went there for the Central Conference in 1970, tried to be fair to the total situation in the places where they served. They had a strong desire to protect the ongoing life of the Church. They may sometimes have failed to take positions that some individuals and groups among their own people and others elsewhere would have liked them to take. But I remember that Asbury and McKendree did not come to grips with the slavery issue in the United States in a way that many Methodists thought they

TRAVELING THE WORLD PARISH WITHOUT SADDLEBAGS

should, part of the reason being that they were so anxious that the Church not be divided."

FIRST TRIP TO EUROPE

When the Shorts journeyed to Europe first in 1954, they went in the company of the great missionary, Bishop Arthur J. Moore. At that time he headed the Geneva Area, and Bishop Odd Hagen at Stockholm was superintending the work in Northern Europe. Roy preached at both Norwegian and Swedish Conferences. In Finland he had an unforgettable experience with an interpreter, Dubrovin by name. He and a Finnish nurse were the only persons in the church, besides Roy and Louise, who understood English.

Roy told a story from his childhood including mention of a porch that "ran beside his mother's kitchen door." That sent the interpreter and the nurse to the English-Finnish dictionary, to discover what a porch was and how it could run. Roy points out a moral: "Then and there I learned something about speaking through an interpreter when the hearers' experiences are different from your own. Unfamiliar terms, colloquial words and phrases represent a hopeless stumbling block."[4]

At the Belgian Conference the Shorts discovered that all the churches except one were in Belgium, and this one was in France. "How did this happen?" Roy asked, and the pastor said, "We just flowed over." Roy called this the secret of successful missions work—flow over and identify with need wherever it is.[5]

MISSIONS OVERFLOWING IN SOUTHEAST ASIA

In Singapore and Sarawak the Shorts visited new people and eyebrow-lifting places under the guidance of such seasoned missionaries as Bishop Hobart Amstutz and his wife

Celeste.⁶ They went up the Rajang River and spent a thrilling night in a longhouse, with the Ibans in Sarawak. Louise wrote: "The beauty of the lands and waters stay constantly in our thoughts, but we prize most the memories of the people we met. There were the three-year missionaries with their amazing enthusiasm, the veterans with their Christian philosophy and unswerving hope, and the maturing local leadership. All this lifted our spirits. The welcome given us by the humble Iban people troubles your heart, and makes you pray that the Christian gospel will get to them fast enough before other 'gospels' alienate them."

From Bangkok the Shorts went on to Burma on this first of their world-circling trips for missions. Roy preached in the Scots Cathedral, a beautiful old building that spoke volumes about the old days of the British Empire, and a trip upriver into the interior brought frightening glimpses of the new times coming. After they came home and told the story a generous layman gave them $40,000 to use for special gifts to missions. It was divided four ways: $10,000 for Bishop Newell S. Booth's work in Africa, $10,000 for the theological seminary in Sarawak, $10,000 to establish a reading room in Pakistan, and the last $10,000 was divided into smaller amounts for many other projects.

The overflow of Chinese refugees from Communist oppression gave new warnings of the possible shape of things to come among the crowded Asians, trying to make a decision between Christianity and Communism in one of its several forms. They were to learn more later, as the Marxist teachings spread worldwide.

LAST: KOREA, TAIWAN AND HONG KONG

The Short's visit to Korea came a few years later on a special assignment from the Council of Bishops in 1971;

and they stopped to see how Bishop Otto and Frances Nall were getting on with their four-year stint (1968-72) in the Chinese-speaking Provisional Annual Conferences that Bishop Ralph A. Ward had started among the refugees from Communist oppression in Mainland China.

For the first time in his life, Roy had a hospital experience, and that was, fortunately, at the famed Severance Hospital in Seoul. He came to his Taiwan appointment on time. While Frances and Louise rose at 4 o'clock to celebrate the birthday of the Great Sage at a Confucian temple (it was National Teachers Day), the two bishops met with Dr. Chou Lien Hwa, Baptist Chaplain to the President and Madame Chiang Kai-shek. His appraisal of the Taiwan relationship to the nations of Asia was utterly frank and immensely helpful.

The next day there was a meal with President Joseph K. Twanmoh, of Soochow University, founded by Methodist missionaries in 1900 and chartered in the state of Tennessee. When freed from a Japanese prison, Bishop Ward, who had been elected by the China Conference, brought Soochow out of exile in Chungking, West China, and led in re-establishing the school, with American help, in Taipei, on Taiwan. The university and the church grew up together. And during the Nalls' stay Soochow rose from 1,600 students to 4,000. Its status, first as a college of liberal arts in the city of Soochow, then as a law school in Shanghai, before the exile in Chungking, and last as a full-fledged university with departments of liberal arts, music, science, business and, of course, law was a present-day miracle. By 1980 it had 9,500 students.

The Nalls were not sure whether or not the Shorts had come to see that the Council of Bishops' representatives were getting plenty to eat, learning some Chinese, taking care of the board's missionaries, staying out of jail, and, above all, identifying with the people. The Shorts seemed delighted with plans for autonomy, under the requirements set forth in the

Discipline. And when the Nalls went home at Easter time, 1972, to retire, both Hong Kong and Taiwan were self-directing, self-propagating, self-supporting churches. Both continued to welcome missionaries.[7] And, at this writing, they are making progress towards the harder ideals of self-denial and self-sacrifice.

When the history of the Christian effort in China from 1900 to 1980 is written, the significance of recent events will become better understood. With the qualities of both a philosophical and a religious people, the Chinese, wherever they live, will make their own contribution to the Christianity of the tomorrows. They are one fifth of the world's population and always everywhere unmistakably Chinese. They will make their distinctive and unique witness, not in spite of, but because of their Chineseness.[8]

TRAVELING THE WORLD PARISH
WITHOUT SADDLEBAGS

NOTES—SHORT AND LONG

1. The quotation is from a paper, "The Itinerant Ministry," which Bishop Short wrote for the bishops. See also E. Dale Dunlap's "The System of Itineracy in American Methodism—an Historical Essay."
2. Years ago, the Methodist Episcopal Church was accustomed to appointing new bishops to serve a four-year term in some foreign mission field. This practice was dropped for a variety of reasons, and the plan of two-month visits, with detailed reports of the work was adopted. The bishops get their own impressions, at variance with tourists on the one hand and missionary leaders on the other. These accounts make interesting reading.
3. Bishop Ferdinand Sigg, Swiss Methodist in charge of the far-flung Geneva Area, coined the phrase at the 1952 General Conference. The Shorts met him in his own Area when they visited Europe in 1954.
4. Of the Methodist Church in Helsinki, Finland, Louise wrote: "The pastor is a very competent person who served at the front. The Finns have much pine and birch, and that has saved them. They call it 'green gold' because all the world needs wood and pulp. Not long ago the last of their war debt to Russia was paid. The Finns say: 'We will not allow ourselves to be ruined by fear. The Lord's will for us will prevail.' "
5. Of churches in Berlin's East Zone, Louise wrote to friends in Nashville: "Nothing can be brought in except by air and construction is very slow. Our churches have reminded me of our jonquils at home. They seemed buried and dead, yet in the spring they push their heads up, sometimes at first a little lopsided, but at least they are coming through. We saw one new church building in East Berlin and one in the West. Others were in rented places or repaired old structures."

6. The bishops sent Bishops Richard C. Raines and Short to the Judicial Council to see whether that body would reconsider its decision in the Alejandro case. In this case the Judicial Council took the position that a Central Conference where there was term episcopacy and the bishop was not reelected he was no longer a member of the Council of Bishops when his term expired. Also affected were Bishop Amstutz, Bishop Archer, and Bishop Balloch. All four had been elected for a term by a Central Conference. (See chapter 19, "The Bishops and the Councils.")

7. Currently there are a dozen United Methodist missionaries in Taiwan, all in educational work, including Wesley Girls High School in whose teachers' residence the Nalls lived.

8. A broader perspective in the understanding of mission in the total cultural and political context of China is needed. As John Fairbank, noted China scholar, has said in *Christianity and Crisis* for June 27, 1966: "Mission boards are by nature interested in their internal history and in biography, the achievements of individuals who have gone before or who have seen the light. But they seem surprisingly uninterested in the historical influence of mission on the social scene. To leave this broader subject unstudied is to slight the memory of preceding generations and to let the present one labor under a stigma that is undeserved."

9
CUBA AND CHANGES IN THE WORLD CHURCH

*I*n 1948 the Methodist Church in Cuba celebrated its 50th anniversary. The Southeastern Jurisdictional Conference had left Bishop Costen J. Harrell, of the Birmingham Area, in charge through the celebration. Roy Short, with Cuba added to the Jacksonville Area, held his first Cuba Conference in 1949.

The mission, one of the fields that had been opened by the Methodist Episcopal Church, South, was made up of smaller churches, for the most part, with some primary schools and several colleges. While most other denominations had concentrated their work in a few centers, Methodism was scattered over the island from one end to the other. Cuba, the "Pearl of the Antilles," with the adjacent Isle of Pines,[1] covers 44,000 square miles. Immediately Roy started visiting the churches and reached practically all of them.

He found a faithful band of missionaries and Cuban workers furnishing the leadership. All ministerial salaries were the same—just under $100 a month, with a small supplement for each child in the family, paid from a common fund to which churches contributed according to their ability. The lowest payment by a local church was $17 and the highest was $100 a month. Only one church was self-supporting.

Roy found that it was the responsibility of the bishop to

raise approximately a quarter of each pastor's salary, with much financial aid for the schools and colleges. He says: "I found this to be a frightening responsibility, but there were many people in the Florida Conference, and elsewhere, who were willing to help me and the Cubans." Hear him describe his task:

"I found that the real job in Cuba was to infuse a new spirit into all aspects of the work. In our second year we had an evangelistic campaign throughout the length and breadth of the island. It was led by Dr. Harry Denman.[2] He brought a company of preachers from the United States, and they preached in the churches and visited in the community. The plan was highly successful. We followed it the year after, and the year after that. It became a pattern for similar campaigns in other mission fields.

"Perhaps the best loved leader among the Cuban pastors in my day was Dr. Angel E. Fuster, pastor at Santa Clara and superintendent of the Santa Clara district. He had been a Crusade Scholar and was highly qualified as a leader, with many gifts and graces. He was a member of the General Board of Christian Social Concerns, 1960-64. He became administrative assistant for Cuba under Bishop James W. Henley in 1961. When there were difficulties with the Castro regime, he remained at his post and was able to keep the Methodists together."

AN INSULAR VIEW OF CASTRO

Roy arrived in Havana on his second tour of duty only a few days after Fidel Castro took over. Bishop Branscomb had died in January, 1959, and the College of Bishops of the Southeastern Jurisdiction asked Roy to supervise the year and a half remaining in the 1956-60 quadrennium. He had already been asked to add responsibility for the Louisville

CUBA AND CHANGES IN THE WORLD CHURCH

Conference because of the illness of Bishop William Watkins. This meant that the Short list of Conference duties was long—Holston, Tennessee, Kentucky and Cuba Mission. "In addition to the secretaryship of the Council of Bishops, this made the heaviest year of my episcopal experience," he explains. He has this word about the new head of government, Fidel Castro:

"In Cuba I found at first considerable enthusiasm for Castro among the missionaries, preachers and lay people. Many saw in him a new ray of hope. At the Conference in 1959 there was real eagerness and hopefulness. The Conference decided to have a Cuba for Christ Campaign and to raise $20,000 a year for the expansion of the Church.

"It was decided that the Conference would move into the rugged Sierra Maestra region, which was a Castro stronghold. While Conference was in session a team was sent on an exploratory visit; although I could not go, Louise did. One of the most effective men was made district superintendent in that new field.

"By the time of the 1960 Annual Conference there was much disillusionment with the regime that had seemed to offer so much promise the year before. Many complained about the policy of intervention, under which the state would take over land or a business without explanation or immediate compensation. Also, there was mounting objection to the policy of surveillance becoming so complete as to include whole areas block by block. Violations of personal freedom were talked about and gave great concern.

"Clearly, the attitude in this year's Conference was in striking contrast to that of the year before. And this was the last time that I was able to visit the Cuba Conference. My responsibility was continued for one year after 1960, because I was familiar with the situation, and the time had come when contact had been shut off except for international contacts or telephone. Contacts had to be made by correspondence or overseas telephone. In 1961 the oversight of the Annual Conference was passed to Bishop James Henley, of the Jacksonville Area."

AN EPISCOPAL ELECTION POSTHUMOUSLY

Of course, Roy, with Florida Methodism and many other parts of the Church, maintained a close interest in Cuba. Because the western section of the island is only 90 miles from Key West, Floridians welcomed every scrap of news they could get concerning the churches on the other side of the straits. Refugees from the Castro regime poured in. Of Dr. Fuster, Roy says:

"The Cubans thought so much of him that, when he died in 1967, they did something that I believe had never been done before. He was visiting Florida and died as a result of injuries in an auto accident. Some months later, when Cuba Methodism was organized as an autonomous church, the delegates elected him bishop. Then they went on to choose Dr. Armando Rodriguez, who was consecrated by Bishop Alejandro Ruiz of Mexico."[3]

Roy's assignment to Cuba as a foreign mission field, led him to think some long, long thoughts about the whole missionary enterprise outside the boundaries of the United States. As always, he was carefully analytical. He wrote his 1964 memorandum on "The Structure of Methodism Overseas," remembering a black leader's pertinent question, "Overseas from where?"[4]

"Originally the contact of the church at home and the church overseas was almost exclusively the bishop. Sent out by the church at the home base, he not only sought to give inspiration and counsel and presided at Conference sessions, but likewise he found lodged in himself almost exclusively the power of decision.

"Later, with the growth of the Missionary Society and the Board of Missions, a policy emerged under which the bishop and the board worked jointly. Still later, as a newer day in missions began to dawn, the field itself was drawn into the operation of the enterprise through such means as field committees and other devices for fuller local participation."

Warning that "methods we have and are using are part of our success and failure," Roy suggested that careful study be given to the *Discipline* (1960, paragraph 1169) which says that "other agencies shall conduct work in foreign fields only with the consent of and in cooperation with the Board of Missions." He wondered whether the board ought not be encouraged on occasion to call in other agencies of the Church where their particular skills may promise to be helpful. He faced the possibility, even probability, that the churches overseas might want to deal directly with the agencies—educational, medical and evangelistic—of the parent church. He urged a careful attempt at solution of a cluster of such problems "rather than simply allowing younger churches to stumble their way toward solutions."[5]

DISMANTLING A WORLD CHURCH?

Occasional tension between the Board of Missions as an administrative agency and most of the bishops charged with administration in mission fields dates back to a period shortly following the organization of this important board.

In the late sixties there was considerable difference of opinion between certain board executives and some of the bishops about the wisdom of encouraging the dissolution of a world church and encouraging the establishment of autonomous churches. In-depth consultations on the subject were held throughout the Church under the auspices of the Commission on the Structure of Methodism Overseas. Roy linked the bishops with missionary pioneering in a 1964 paper he wrote on structure. He said:

"Our own Methodist Church, which was born in the United States in 1784 had always been, in fact, predominantly a United States church. But now it finds itself with nine or ten Central Conferences, 27 affiliated autonomous churches and several united churches. This significant development of the church overseas has been the result of a process stretching back almost 150 years."

He writes of churches that, for a variety of reasons, "developed independently" of the Church to which they were related. He continued:

"The most striking illustration of this at the beginning of the current missionary movement was, of course, William Taylor, ardent but irregular Methodist that he was, who very largely on his motion and by sheer strength of his own willpower, established work on three continents which subsequently became part of Methodism overseas.

"The efforts of the Board of Bishops (of the Methodist Episcopal Church) to induce him to follow some patterns of regularity make exceedingly interesting reading, climaxed as they are by his locating in order to be free, and his being elected to the episcopacy as a layman—the only person so elected in Methodism. Even after he became bishop in Africa he still resisted any control by his brother bishops.

"Bishop Taylor was the only person who dared to act independently in planting the Church overseas. Perhaps there is something in the very makeup of a person sufficiently bold to answer a missionary call which makes that person chafe under restraint and quick to act on his own impulses. Only God himself knows how many Methodist congregations have

CUBA AND CHANGES IN THE WORLD CHURCH

been begun overseas, as well as at home, not as a result of strategic church planning, but as an effect of independent missionary action. There is something noble and glorious about such action."

In this paper Roy had some embarrassing questions to ask of the leaders who were entertaining an image of a Church which must prove to be largely an American rather than a world church. He did not welcome the idea, even in a time when the spirit of nationalism was sweeping the world, that Methodists should abandon the world parish idea.

The Committee on the Structure of Methodism Overseas called a worldwide meeting at Atlantic City in 1970. There was spirited debate and sharp division of opinion, with most of the churches of Asia and Latin America and the Central Conference people of Europe and Africa generally finding themselves ranged on opposite sides. In the 1972 *Discipline* the duties of the Committee on the Structure of Methodism Overseas were passed over to the Commission on Central Conference Affairs. The expensive Conference of Bishops from worldwide Methodism was scrapped, but it now shows signs of being restored in some form.

As secretary of the Council of Bishops (see the next chapter) Roy Short saw the development of Provisional Annual Conferences and Central Conferences at close range. He served five and a half years in Cuba. He presided at several Conferences in Europe and Asia. He was sent by the Council of Bishops on special missions to Rhodesia, Korea, the Philippines, Brazil, Chile, India and Liberia. He wondered whether the Board of Global Ministries, under its new structure, would become "more and more a cooperative agency so far as other parts of the world are concerned rather than, as at present, an essentially administrative agency. Perhaps that is what maturity in mission would demand."

CENTRAL CONFERENCE BISHOPS ARE BISHOPS, TOO

Roy never made any distinction among bishops elected by General Conference (and he knew the old-timers), others by Jurisdictional Conferences and those elected by Central Conferences. As secretary of the Council, he frequently counseled with Bishop Ole Borgen, who has pioneered the vigorous development of the Central Conferences, with 4,124 churches and 528,000 members at the last count. There are currently fifteen active Central Conference bishops and ten retired.

Bishop Ole E. Borgen's name is not only first on the alphabetical list, but also first among equals in helping Central Conference bishops to understand what are their rights and duties under the *Discipline*.[6]

Of Roy's help Ole says:

"He is supportive in indicating what can be done strategically, but he does not, as he could not, sponsor proposals of the Central Conference leaders. The only direct advice he ever gave me was this: 'Don't get involved in anything that requires a decision by the Judicial Council!' I have not found him nostalgic about the past, but he is, in my view, cautious about seizing the promises of the future. Frequently I have heard him say, 'That can be done sometime, but not now.' "

There is more about Roy's role as secretary of the Council of Bishops in the next chapter.

CUBA AND CHANGES IN THE WORLD CHURCH

NOTES—SHORT AND LONG

1. The enthusiasm of the missionaries is indicated by Carl Stewart's whimsical rating of three excellent places in ascending order: Heaven, Cuba, the Isle of Pines. This was pre-Castro, of course.
2. Heroic Harry Denman had an unsuppressible desire to evangelize certain parts of the "foreign field." But everything in this part of the world was considered to be reserved for the Board of Missions. At first he turned down offers, then accepted, first in Scandinavia, then in Asia, especially in Malaysia and Korea, where he had a most successful mission at Ewha Womans University.
3. Dr. Fuster's widow now works on the staff of the Florida Conference at Lakeland, in the department of audio-visual aids.
4. The bishop was Bertram W. Doyle of the Christian Methodist Episcopal Church, and the meeting was the executive committee of the World Methodist Council at Kingston, Jamaica. Somebody wondered why so many meetings had to be held "overseas."
5. These quotations are from a lengthy paper that Roy wrote for the Structure Committee report to the General Conference of 1964. See also references to missionaries in chapter 14, entitled, "Bishops in Political Crises."
6. Bishop Borgen is also pianist for the Council of Bishops who, regrettably, no longer sing the "Bishops' Hymn," "Beloved, we are the sons of God." Older bishops, with a sense of humor, used to ask Jurisdictional Conferences to please elect more tenors.

10
BISHOPS ARE PEOPLE—
ONE PEOPLE

*B*ack in 1956, Bishop G. Bromley Oxnam, assigned by the Northeastern Jurisdictional Conference to the Washington Area, asked to be relieved as secretary of the Council of Bishops. He had served for 16 years.[1] During this time he had been the mastermind of the Council, preparing the agenda for the meetings, writing countless letters and attending to endless details. Even the president did not usually know what was to come up at the meetings until he saw what the secretary had placed on his desk.

The presidency changed from year to year, with the gavel handed over at the spring meeting,[2] but the secretary was chosen for the quadrennium. The president presided but Bishop Oxnam, as secretary, dominated the meeting by the very strength of his energetic personality. He wrote shorthand and gave careful and wise attention to every item of business. He had, moreover, the ability to analyze a situation quickly and to come up with proposals for working through a difficulty.

Roy remembers him as "the soul of courtesy, but an impatient person; and if he felt that a brother bishop was not saying anything really important, he would rise in his place at the table and remain standing until the speaker took the hint and sat down."

BISHOPS ARE PEOPLE—
ONE PEOPLE

"The bishops all appreciated his wisdom and usually deferred to him, and in a considerable measure, allowed him to control and guide the Council. Because he was having certain health problems, he asked to be relieved of the secretarial duties. The bishops wondered what they could possibly do without him." Roy tells the story:

"For eight years I had sat quietly in the Council. I had seldom spoken, for I do not consider myself to be a good debater. (Actually, I was not even asked to lead a devotional until after I retired.) Bishop Titus Lowe and Bishop Arthur Moore passed the word around that I had been an Annual Conference secretary for 17 years, and on the second ballot I was elected. Bishop Oxnam moved that my election be for a single year, since I was untried, but after I had taken the minutes for a year it was he who moved that my election be extended for the quadrennium, 1956-60. During my second year Bishop Oxnam himself was president of the Council."

Roy adds: "No president was ever kinder, or more thoughtful or easier to work with. And it turned out that I served as secretary until I retired in 1972. I must confess that, sitting in the Council, I had reacted to the pattern followed by Bishop Oxnam in the secretaryship, but I never mentioned this to any brother bishop. When I was elected I determined thereafter that I would try to be only a recording secretary.

"To this end I made some changes in procedure: I sent the usual letter to all my colleagues, asking them to name matters that they wanted on the agenda, and I consulted with the president before giving them a place there. I asked him to select the devotional leaders and others having special assignments.

"I arranged to meet privately with the president before the opening of each session so that he would be thoroughly familiar with whatever had been scheduled for consideration. With the help of the United Methodist Publishing House, I introduced bound copies of the agenda for the meetings and similar copies of the minutes afterwards. Until that time only loose-leaf pages had been provided for the bishops."

During his long term as secretary, Roy performed a feat that left preachers and lay people as well as his brother bishops and their wives breathless. Wherever the bishops were seated, the secretary would rise in his place and call the name of each bishop and his wife, indicating the Area where each one was serving. This particularly impressed the bishops from outside the United States, whose names are sometimes difficult for an English-speaking person to remember and pronounce. At such gatherings Roy felt that the applause was more a tribute to the warm fellowship of the Council than to his own memory.

REPORTS, REPORTS, MORE REPORTS

In times past it was said that preachers went to Annual Conference to exchange sermons and bishops went to their college and council meetings to swap preachers and pass resolutions. All this is part of the mythology of Methodism. In these latter days most of the mornings, afternoons and evenings are consumed with hearing reports, some of which come in book-length, typed manuscripts. Many of the boards and agencies try their plans on the bishops, on the plausible theory that if the bishops do not generally approve a program dreamed up in bureaucratic offices there is not much chance of getting it before the Annual Conferences.

For the past eight years the Council of Bishops has had four standing committees on which all bishops, including those retired and those from Areas in all parts of the world, sit for committee discussions that take at least half a day. These standing committees have "concerns"—pastoral, educational, administrative and relational. (The first three deal

BISHOPS ARE PEOPLE—
ONE PEOPLE

with interests that are fairly obvious; Relational Concerns has to do with matters of relationships between the Church and governments, other denominations and philanthropic organizations, councils of churches and such bodies.)

Other reports come from the Church's councils—finance and administration, judicial and ministries.

The colleges—the name given the bishops, active and retired, in each of the five Jurisdictions—always meet for a morning or afternoon of the semiannual meetings, as well as two or three other times during the year. These are regional meetings—Northeastern, Southeastern, North Central, South Central and Western, with all the Central Conference bishops in an additional college. Each college is represented on the Executive Committee by its president and two other members. The president, past-president, president-elect and secretary of the Council are also on this committee, whose increasingly frequent meetings have expedited the Council's work.

IF YOU WANT TO PRESENT SOMETHING—

Whether you are a bishop or not, the way to get a matter before the Council of Bishops for some action is to submit a paper to the Council's secretary and have it referred to one of the standing committees, on one of which each bishop, active or retired, sits. These standing committees do the screening for the whole Council. The Council has so increased in size that the committees themselves are now sizeable bodies. Roy comments: "At a recent meeting the Committee on Administrative Concerns had only three fewer members present than were on the whole Board of Bishops of the Methodist Episcopal Church at the time of Methodist union in 1939."

The committees on administrative, pastoral, educational and relational concerns canvass all matters before them and make appropriate recommendations to the Council as a whole for final action. Technically, any matter that a bishop deems important may be brought to the whole Council, and moving the "previous question" is discountenanced, but the program has become so crowded that a proposal has little chance unless it passes through the screening process.

Roy makes a confession that some bishops have taken as an example: "I am so constituted that I cannot trust myself to think quickly and express myself readily while I am on my feet. So, long ago, I developed the habit of anticipating what might come up at a future session and writing out my thinking on that subject. I try to do my homework and have a paper or two in my pocket in case those particular matters come up. Of course, I followed the same procedure after I became the secretary.

"Bishop Oxnam used to ask us, 'Where is the point of decision?' and then he would urge us to 'get to that point if you want action. If bishops do not come to that point, they will not be thought of as leaders who can actually lead.' "

Roy thinks that the Executive Committee is a most important part of the Council's equipment. "However," he warns, "the committee must guard against making decisions in any matters not referred to it by the Council except in extreme emergencies. It must not become a substitute for the Council." Furthermore, Roy points out that there have been some bishops who have been in the Council for some time but who have never held office or served on the Executive Committee.[3]

Succeeding secretaries of the Council have made other helpful suggestions.[4]

CORPORATENESS IN THE COUNCIL

While the bishops do not elect each other, they have a natural interest in those who, by the vote of both

BISHOPS ARE PEOPLE—
ONE PEOPLE

clergy and lay members of the Jurisdictional Conferences, may be added to the episcopal ranks. Bishop Jack Tuell has probably spoken for all in saying:

"Bishops are expected to lead. . . . The historic and ecclesiastical discussions of the episcopacy add much weight to the assertion that the bishops are the natural leaders of the Church, both as individual bishops and in their corporate capacity as a Council of Bishops."[5]

Bishop W. Ralph Ward adds: "I am confident that I speak for all in the Council when I say that no one who has been working *on the four concerns* of the standing committees expects a corporateness that will blot out individualism, personal styles of leadership, unique and properly differing capabilities and skills, making us, as it were, in the Council a company of faceless persons, seemingly the product of the same cookie cutter. . . .

"We affirm this concept of diversity of gifts and graces within the unity of the Council. We affirm the fact of pluralism in leadership style and official administration. It is expected that, in the Council, those who are elected to the episcopacy will be themselves and not imitators of others. . . . Withal, both by the *Discipline* and tradition, we are more than a string of individuals bearing an historic title. We are called into a Council of Bishops, and the Church has a right to expect us to bear witness to that kind of identity."

The role of the secretary is still in the process of being defined. The fact that Roy Short had to give Council matters more than half his time (and without a full-time secretary) has led some bishops to suggest that there ought to be a bishop set apart for this heavy responsibility. In 1968 the Council reached the conclusion that it was asking too much to expect a bishop to serve as secretary and at the same time administer an Area. By secret ballot the Council favored the plan and it was endorsed by the General Conference. But that body insisted that, like a constitutional matter, this should have the approval of two thirds of the Annual Conferences. By informal vote the Council had asked Roy to accept this responsibility, if the proposal were approved. The vote in the Annual Conferences failed to reach the two thirds needed.

A variety of explanation was given, probably the best rooting far back in Methodist beginnings in the United States. In 1808, when Bishop McKendree, the first native American bishop, was chosen, Bishop Asbury noted in his *Journal* that Brother McKendree was elected "assistant bishop." McKendree never acknowledged such subordination. Actually, he had done some things that were not pleasing to the seasoned "apostle of the long road." One was to consult with the presiding elders in making appointments, an idea that later developed into the "cabinet." Another was to present an episcopal address before General Conference, a procedure to which Asbury objected.

Any whispered notion that American Methodism have an "archbishop" or presiding bishop with any status that other bishops do not have has always been quickly quashed. All bishops are on a parity in salaries, housing allowances and pensions for their terms of service as bishops, qualification being made in the case of Central Conference bishops or differences in the economy in places where they serve.

How this affects issues and causes will be examined in succeeding chapters.

BISHOPS ARE PEOPLE—
ONE PEOPLE

NOTES—SHORT AND LONG

1. There is no provision for the election of Council of Bishops leaders, presidents and secretaries by *Disciplinary* rule.
2. The passing of the gavel continues at the spring meeting. The bishops meet, except in the General Conference year, the week after Easter and the week before Thanksgiving. Gossip is that bishops are less needed at home in their Areas when the local churches are in the midst of Christian festival seasons. In General Conference years the bishops convene a week before the Conference, but not in the Conference city.
3. In a 1971 paper on "The Major Problems of the Council of Bishops as seen by the Secretary," Bishop Short pointed out the top priority problem was "to assert, without apology the leadership role assigned to it by the *Discipline*, not only currently but from the beginning." He said that the Church expected "not dominance but positive, constructive leadership." He warned: "The general effect of what is now happening, both with and without our consent, appears to move in the direction of reducing the episcopacy to a largely symbolic episcopacy, functioning chiefly at the Area level and making the Council of Bishops itself a body that is far less than a 'general superintendency.' "
4. Bishop James K. Mathews, currently secretary, has written a paper "On Being the Council of Bishops." He has this to say: "While our episcopacy is protected by the Third Restrictive Rule against being abolished, many feel that our general overseership has been replaced by our function as promoters. To the degree that this is true, we have only ourselves to blame. We can either bog down in trivia or give leadership on larger things—what issues do we want our Church to face together with other churches, in what direction we shall proceed? To matters of such magnitude general superintendents must direct their energies. But we must do it together."

5. The quotations are from a long and exceedingly helpful paper by a task force named by the Executive Committee on "Manifesting Corporateness in the Council of Bishops." It concludes: "Our fathers in the faith have left us magnificent illustrations of episcopal presence and striking examples of leadership through the Council of Bishops. Yet we must be more than traditional in response to the issues of this hour. Yesterday's style of response to the bishops' role in the Church requires more refitting for today."

11

RACISM—PERSONAL AND INSTITUTIONAL

In 1937, when Roy Short was a much traveling, hard working young presiding elder in Kentucky, he was invited to write an article for *The Adult Student*, a Sunday school periodical of the Southern Church. The subject was: "A World Church." The assignment attracted him, he remembers, because "one appeal I felt for union of our Southern Methodism with the Methodist Episcopal Church was that, in the full sense, it was a worldwide church, as the Methodist Episcopal Church, South, was not.

"We were confined largely to the South and Southwest, with fragments in California and the Northwest, even Montana. Our mission work was limited to China, Korea, Brazil, Cuba, Belgium, Czechoslovakia and Poland. We had no Black Conferences, for those we had became the Colored Methodist Episcopal Church, now substituting the word *Christian* for *Colored*." Roy says:

"As I go back and read my article again I note that I was then a young preacher insisting that the Church should be structured without regard to racial differences or national barriers. I did not realize at that time that, actually, I was anticipating much of what I would be concerned about in later years."

Five years afterwards Roy became pastor of the prestigious

St. Paul Church, Louisville, and in the same city Dr. I. R. Sumner was pastor of the large and important Jones Temple, of the Central Jurisdiction. These two Methodist pastors formed a strong friendship and established a working relationship between their two congregations. They began with joint meetings of the young people—sometimes at St. Paul and sometimes at Jones Temple. "And it was something of an advanced step for that day." Roy recalls some steps in his personal pilgrimage on racial understanding:

"When I went to the Upper Room no black person had had a meditation in the periodical, so far as I could discover. I asked Bishop Alexander P. Shaw, who was then senior bishop in the Central Jurisdiction, to prepare a meditation. He did so, and since that day almost countless black writers, as well as authors from most nations of the world have appeared in *The Upper Room.*"

As bishop of the Holston Conference in the early fifties, Roy asked Bishop Edgar A. Love to be with him at a Conference session. "I did not consult with him beforehand, but when we came to a certain point I announced that I was going to ask Bishop Love to take the chair. He was surprised, but he came to the table and presided with the fine skill that he had. Actually, I put him in the chair at precisely the point in the program where, a year before, I had asked Bishop Fred P. Corson, a visitor to our Conference, to preside. Bishop Love told me it was the first time a black bishop had presided at a Conference in the Southeastern Jurisdiction.

"When he handed back the gavel to me the Conference rose to its feet and applauded. Afterwards I received a number of letters from young men—and some from older ones—praising this simple gesture of goodwill."

During the stress and strain of the late fifties and early sixties, Roy read to the Council of Bishops a paper raising the question about what attitude and action the Council should

RACISM—PERSONAL AND INSTITUTIONAL

take, both as individuals and as a group, on race. Following the reading of the paper there was discussion, and a special committee representing all the six Jurisdictions was set up.

Bishop Paul E. Martin of the South Central Jurisdiction was named chairman. The others were: Bishop Charles Golden of the Central Jurisdiction, Bishop Marvin Stuart of the Western, Bishop Richard Raines of the North Central, Bishop W. Ralph Ward of the Northeastern, and Bishop Roy Short of the Southeastern. Roy remembers:

"All of us agreed to surrender our plans for celebration of the Fourth of July and to meet in Chicago to get our work under way. From that time until the elimination of the Central Jurisdiction in 1968 the Council continued to hack away at problems standing in the path of complete elimination of racial discrimination in the life of the Church."[1]

READING THE SIGNS OF THE TIMES

In 1966, the Southeastern Jurisdictional Council met at Jackson, Mississippi, and Bishop Paul N. Garber had been invited to be the principal speaker. When he could not come, Roy was asked to substitute. He used as his text: "You can read the signs in the sky—why can you not read the signs of the times?" (Luke 12:56)

Because the address focused on racial problems, it made the headlines in the newspapers.[2] Roy was invited to speak on the same subject at a number of other meetings in the South.

In 1968, he had the episcopal address at the Jurisdictional Conference. In it he said: "One of the major social problems of the hour comes to particular focus for us in our section of the country; namely, that of the achievement of racial justice and freedom. A large proportion of the population of the Southeast is black. For long years the black and white have lived here side by side; and whether we have always been wise enough to know it or not, we are bound up inextricably in a bundle of life together. What hurts any one of us hurts all of us, and if any one of us is not fully free, none of us is actually free. The time has come now for this to be acknowledged in fact as well as in theory.

"The sweeping revolution of our day is bringing far-reaching changes to the South, as well as to other sections of our land, and to all the world. These changes should be accepted for the progress in human relations that they represent, and the justice and equity which they seek to express."

With the coming of union between The Methodist Church and the Evangelical United Brethren, who had no racial units, the Central Jurisdiction was abolished and half of the Conferences in the entire Southeastern Jurisdiction were merged. The bishops of the Jurisdiction hoped that complete merger shortly thereafter "would not prove an impossible realization within a reasonable limit of time."

In a 1966 report to the Southeastern bishops Roy outlined some of the problems, including the fact that black Methodists needed a "power base" in the Annual Conferences, on the boards and, of course, in the episcopacy. It was clear to Roy that the prayed for end of the Central Jurisdiction would not itself be the cure-all that much impassioned rhetoric promised.

ON SEEING EACH OTHER IN ST. LOUIS

The once popular song about meeting one's friends in St. Louis had a strange relationship when United Methodists gathered there in 1970 for a special General Conference called to perfect union. It came within a hairsbreadth of blowing the new United Methodist Church apart.

Tense moments that had not occurred in Council of Bishops meetings in decades came when, following personal con-

RACISM—PERSONAL
AND INSTITUTIONAL

ferences with youth in their offices across the Church, the Bishops found themselves barricaded in their meeting room at the Jefferson Hotel. One of the black bishops counseled his stunned brethren: "Don't try to be brave and show your manhood by trying to force your way out. They mean business!"

The bishops agreed to hear the youth—most of them white—and then to make plans for additional funds for projects to help the black people. The young protesters wanted money—large amounts—with no strings attached. No promises were made, but arrangements were agreed upon whereby the group might be heard in General Conference session, if they did not attempt to incite violence. They came, surrounded the assembly and stood quietly while their leader, a young preacher from Memphis, gave what turned out to be a strong plea with a reconciling note. It was well received.

By a strange coincidence, Roy had been invited to preach on Sunday morning in famed old Centenary Church, where college students from the North and the South had met together on the eve of the Uniting Conference in 1939 at Kansas City. Centenary Church was well filled that Sunday morning in St. Louis. There were some youth on the ground floor, and in the balcony was a group dressed like frontier people in leather breeches and fringed jackets, with the girls in Mother Hubbard dresses. They turned out to be members of the "Submarine Church."

Soon after the service started it became apparent that some form of demonstration had been planned. In the midst of the first hymn a young man in a long black coat arose and proclaimed, as he came forward to the pulpit, "I have a great sorrow!" When the pastor announced that he could share it after the service, the impromptu preacher insisted on preaching right then and there. He was told that he could say anything he wished, and there would be people to hear him after the worship hour.

Other young people then rose to their feet in various parts of the congregation. The ushers came forward and removed the would-be preacher. A young woman in a red dress—she turned out to be the preacher's wife—came streaking down the aisle. She affirmed that she had the same great sorrow, and she was shocked that a Methodist congregation would not hear a Methodist preacher when he wanted to tell of a burden on his heart.[3]

There was great confusion in the congregation and Roy felt that the service could not proceed. He suggested that the benediction be pronounced and the congregation dismissed. There was no reference to race, and the part of the Submarine Church that surfaced was all white.

There was little of the spirit of reconciliation in the General Conference at St. Louis, and most delegates seemed glad when it adjourned, for lack of a quorum, ahead of schedule.

TWO METHODIST BISHOPS IN THE SAME CITY

In 1960 Bishop Charles Golden, whose father had been a staff member of the Board of Evangelism, was elected and assigned to Nashville. The Central Jurisdiction created that year a new Nashville-Carolina Area, which meant that Roy and the bishop son of his old friend Dr. J. W. Golden would have offices in the same city. When it was clear that there was no commercial space available Roy hoped that a place could be found in the new Publishing House building where his own office was located. Roy puts it this way:

"I felt that something needed to be done in order that Bishop Golden might be accommodated. I was sure that I could not myself remain in a luxurious office while my brother bishop in the same city had less than adequate quarters. Therefore, I took it upon myself to talk to Scarritt College, the Board of Evangelism and the Board of Educa-

PHOTOGRAPHS OF THE LIFE AND WORK OF
Roy Hunter Short

PHOTO BY WILEY PERRY

Louise and Roy Short before his portrait in parlor named for him, Bishops' Hall, Emor University.

(ABOVE) Marcus Lindsey United Methodist Church, Louisville, Kentucky. Various members of Bishop Short's family have been in this church for more than a hundred years. Bishop Short was baptized here; joined the church as a child; taught Sunday school here; was licensed to preach here; married Louise here on September 1, 1926; and was pastor here 1928-30. The church still carries his name on the roll. (BELOW) Bishop Short's local preacher's license issued by the licensing committee of the Louisville District on September 18, 1920.

LOCAL PREACHER'S LICENSE.

The bearer thereof, *Roy Hunter Short*, having been duly recommended by the Quarterly Conference of *Marcus Lindsey Station*, and having been examined, as the Discipline directs, by a Licensing committee of the District Conference of *Louisville* District of the *Louisville* Annual Conference of the Methodist Episcopal Church, South, is hereby authorized to preach the gospel, according to the rules and regulations of said Church.

Signed, in behalf of said District Conference,

S. J. Thompson, President

J. A. Arnold, Secretary of the Committee

Date, *September 18* 1920.

(LEFT, TOP) Alert, even at 10 months, Roy Hunter Short looks out on his world. (CENTER LEFT) Bishop Short and his youngest son, Riley, at ordination *(1960)* in Holston Conference. (ABOVE) St. Paul Church, Louisville, Roy Short's last pulpit. (BELOW) Shorts, Roy and Louise, with Hunter behind Roy, Murray, and Riley on their last Sunday at St. Paul Church.

Roy Short and Louise Baird when they started going together.

PHOTO BY EARLE H. MAC LEDD

(ABOVE, LEFT) Bishop Short and Bishop Earl G. Hunt, Jr., at installation in Nashville *(1976)*. The ceremony was held at West End United Methodist Church. (ABOVE RIGHT) Bishop and Mrs. Short at time of bishop's election.

(ABOVE) College of Bishops in Southeastern Jurisdiction in 1948, when Bishop Short and Bishop Franklin became part of it. *(front row, from left)* Clare Purcell, Marvin Franklin, Roy Short, Walter W. Peele; *(back row)* Paul Kern, Arthur Moore, Costen J. Harrell, William T. Watkins. Bishop Short is the only member of the group living in 1979.

(ABOVE) Bishop Short's Cuba cabinet in 1951: *(front row)* Maurice Dailey, Bishop Short, Carl Stewart; *(back row)* Louis D'Arce, Moises Boudet, and Garfield Evans. (BELOW) Bishop Short and his guest Dr. Harry Denman of Board of Evangelism stand before oxcart loaded in cane field for mill. Despite competition of beet sugar, cane remains Cuba's best agricultural product, dominant since eighteenth century.

(ABOVE) Florida's Conference-wide program in 1951 shows bishop's zeal for evangelism, which he always links with missions.

PHOTO BY DUANE PERKINS

(ABOVE) Bishop Short with his first cabinet in the Florida Conference: *(from left)* H. H. Waller, J. W. Blake, H. W. Blackburn, Bishop Short, A. Fred Turner, John Stradley, Schuler Peele and Paul Fletcher. (BELOW) Bishop Short preaches in Upper Room Chapel before wood carving of Leonardo da Vinci's *The Last Supper.*

PHOTO BY ELDRED REANEY

(AT LEFT) Bishop and Mrs. Short embark from the *Queen Mary* on first European visitation in 1954. (ABOVE) Bishop Short leads "hat game" during fun night at a cabinet retreat, after a busy day of cabinet work.

PHOTO BY PHOTO ARTS

Bishop and Mrs. Short are greeted at Miami on return from Latin American visitation in 1951 to Peru and Brazil.

PHOTO BY DON SMALL

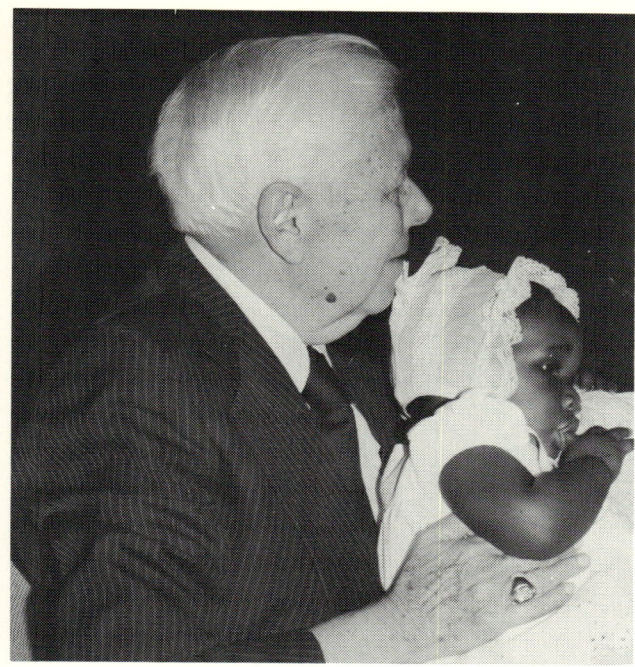

(AT LEFT) Bishop Short holds little Joy Moon, daughter of Rev. and Mrs. James L. Moon, at Tennessee Conference in Clarksville, Tennessee, in 1979.

(ABOVE) Bishop Short puts trowel of mortar to cornerstone of new First Church building at Orlando, Florida. It is his first cornerstone laying as bishop. Others in picture: *(from left)* District Superintendent Paul Fletcher, Pastor John Branscomb *(later bishop),* and retired Bishop John Gowdy.

(RIGHT) Bishop Short and Dr. D. T. Niles, leader of Methodist Church of Ceylon *(Sri Lanka).* He made principle speech at World Methodist Conference in 1968. (LEFT) Bishop Edward Tullis, formerly of Kentucky Conference and Bishop Short.

(ABOVE) Consecration of Bishop Stephen Nagbe *(front row, center)* in Cape Palmas, Liberia, as first Liberian-born bishop. Previous bishop was Prince A. Taylor, standing at new bishop's left. Bishop S. U. Barbieri and John Wesley Shungu also stand in front row. All were entertained by President Tubman at his summer palace.

PHOTO BY JACK GUNTER

(ABOVE) Bishop Short and Rev. David B. Sargeant stand with reverent attention before stone placed on spot where old Fountain Head Meeting House stood, and where first session of Tennessee Conference met in 1812. Bishops Francis Asbury and William McKendree presided here years ago. (BELOW) As resident bishop in Nashville *(1952-60),* Bishop Short presides at 150th anniversary session in McKendree Church.

PHOTO BY BOB RAY

(ABOVE) Bishop Short with Bishop William C. Martin in a round of speaking engagements in 1949, both guests of Bishop Clifford Northcott of the Wisconsin Area. (BELOW) Bishop Short, with folded arms, listens to enthusiastic Filipino singing.

(RIGHT) at Southeastern Jurisdictional Conference in Junaluska *(1964),* Bishop Short chairs body, using gavel from wood of house in which he was born, a presentation made by Harry Short *(not a relative),* his successor as editor of *The Kentucky Methodist.* (ABOVE) Bishop Short presides at 1964 General Conference in Pittsburgh.

PHOTO BY COLLINS/COOLEY

(ABOVE) Bishop Short's desk in handsome new building of United Methodist Publishing House at 203 Eighth Avenue South, Nashville. Previously, he occupied office at 810 Broadway. (BELOW) Episcopal residence in Nashville, dedicated in 1954.

PHOTO BY RIE GADDIS

(ABOVE) Judge Orso W. Stanley represents Roy's native state in awarding Kentucky Colonel's certificate. (LEFT) Louise and Roy honored by Holston Conference.

(ABOVE) President Earl G. Hunt, Jr., *(back to camera)* of Emory and Henry College confers *(in 1958)* degree of doctor of canon laws. The degree *(somewhat rare in American church circles)* refers to body of Council canons or pronouncements ratified by church councils since sixteenth century.

PHOTO BY PAN AMERICAN WORLD AIRWAYS

(ABOVE) Planeful of evangelists arrive at Havana airport ready for work in 1952 Cuba campaign. (BELOW) Bishop Short with Bishop Arthur J. Moore at Belmont Church in Nashville in 1962.

PHOTO BY BOB RAY

Louise and Roy Short at time of retirement in 1972. They chose to live in Nashville, where he served 1952-64.

tion, with the hope of finding office room for the two of us.

"Scarritt did not find it possible to reply, but Dr. John O. Gross of the Board of Education and Dr. Harry Denman of the Board of Evangelism said that they would manage to find something in their buildings for the bishop. The Board of Evangelism had a very attractive room available. The Board of Education was under pressure for space but offered to convert what had been a women's lounge into an office.

"I said to Bishop Golden, 'You make the choice. If you go to the Board of Evangelism, I'll go to the Board of Education, or the other way around if that is your wish.' He chose the Board of Evangelism; we both made out very well."

Although there has been some discussion in the Church about whether bishops should "office" in any board headquarters, Roy remained with the Board of Education until the end of his assignment in Nashville. He continued a friendly relationship with the United Methodist Publishing House where he had earlier had his office. In 1968 Bishop Golden was assigned to the San Francisco Area.

The black bishops, going back to Matthew W. Clair and Robert E. Jones, both elected in the Methodist Episcopal Church in 1920, have always made their full contribution to the Council of Bishops, and have enjoyed its complete confidence.

Sixteen black bishops have been elected by General and Jurisdictional Conferences in the United States, and seven by Central Conferences. Bishop Prince A. Taylor was the first black bishop to serve as President of the Council of Bishops, elected in 1964 at Pittsburgh. Bishop James S. Thomas read the Episcopal Address in 1976, and Bishop Roy C. Nichols, who has given special attention to strengthening the ethnic minority churches, was chosen President in 1980.

NOTES—SHORT AND LONG

1. In November, 1954, the bishops, in their regular meeting, passed a resolution commending the Supreme Court decision of May in the same year. It mentioned statements in the Social Creed and the Episcopal Address adopted by the 1952 General Conference. The message said: "The Supreme Court itself recognized that such a ruling brought with it difficulties of enforcement and thereby made provision for sufficient time to implement the decision. The declaration of the decision was made in the magnificent home of the Supreme Court, but the ultimate success of the ruling will be determined in the hearts of the people of the nation. Thus the Church is furnished with an unequaled opportunity to provide leadership during this period in support of the principles involved in the action of the court. We accept this responsibility. . . ."

2. When the bishops met in Detroit the press was eager for news. Some 200 reporters waited outside the meeting room when the bishops' press officer emerged.

3. Readers who want a more complete account of this dramatic incident may consult the files of the *South Carolina Christian Advocate* of the time.

12
SEXISM AND THE STATUS OF WOMEN

*R*oy's and Louise's partnership in their home and in all phases of the Church's life has had a determining effect on their attitudes on many questions and subjects. Louise has always been greatly interested in church affairs and in questions before the Church. She has been active in church life, but more concerned to encourage women in holding church office than in taking office herself, although she has been an officer at times.

Roy says that there were a number of factors that helped shape his thinking with reference to womanhood and the Church. Hear him:

"There was my mother, who was exceedingly active at church—present whenever the church door was open, a faithful singer in the choir, and a fully participating member of the Ladies Aid, the Home Missionary Society and Foreign Missionary Society, too.[1] She was also superintendent of the home department of the Sunday school. She was quite conscious of the fact that, at her point in time, women could not be members of the official board or delegates to the District, Annual or General Conferences.

"There was also my first Sunday school teacher, an ardent Woman's Christian Temperance Union worker, a missionary enthusiast and a strong advocate of woman's suffrage. She paid much attention to me individually as well as in the Sunday school class, where I heard her speak of her concerns so often and so forcibly. All this registered fully on my youthful mind.

"There were the deaconesses at Wesley House, whose classes I attended regularly as a child, and who were a great help to me in many ways. They always wore the deaconess uniform and represented the highest recognition of a special office for women then recognized by Southern Methodism.

"There was Miss Belle Bennett, head of the women's work in the Church South, with whom I had the privilege of spending a long Sunday afternoon on one occasion. By her very presence, grace and dignity, as well as by what she said, she made an unforgettable impression upon me, and let me see that no place in the Church should be beyond its womanhood."[2]

Roy was a member of three General Conferences, where he regularly voted for clergy rights for women. He says: "I was proud that he was a fellow Kentuckian in the 1956 General Conference who offered a single-sentence amendment that settled the matter for all time. As an active bishop I found no problem in placing women preachers that I did not find in placing men preachers. Sometimes, however, it was harder to sell the appointment to the women of the congregation than to the men. Almost all the women preachers with whom I dealt did satisfactory work and were well received in their charges."

MONEY FOR THE TRINKETS

"Some of them were interesting and creative personalities," Roy remembers. "I recall particularly a Kentucky woman whom I assigned as pastor on a hard circuit in North Florida. The district superintendent went to hold his first Quarterly Conference. She made her report saying: 'I have

SEXISM AND THE STATUS OF WOMEN

raised so much for the pastor's salary, and so much for the district superintendent, so much for World Service and so much for the trinkets.'

"The superintendent scratched his head and said: 'That's fine, but what are the trinkets?' She said: 'There are so many other things that you asked me to raise money for, and I couldn't begin to explain them to my people—so I just lump them all together and say, "Please give me so much for the trinkets." ' "

Roy thinks the women have done very well in remembering hunger and many other causes that used to get small parts of the World Service dollar, if anything. Some of these are important causes, little needs that have become major causes.

In his first quadrennium as bishop when he had the work in Cuba he was particularly impressed by his women preachers. They comprised one sixth of the Conference membership. Almost all of them served in rural areas, where they lived simply as the people lived, and they carried on their heroic ministry on horseback.[3] Roy adds:

"I had a great desire to appoint a woman district superintendent and I proposed this as early as 1951, but the woman preacher I approached in the matter asked to be excused.

"Unquestionably, the first woman appointed district superintendent was Augusta Robinett, of Medan, Indonesia. Maud Jensen, wife of Kristian who was one of six Methodist missionaries imprisoned by Communists in Kaesong, Korea, and repatriated by way of Moscow, was the first woman member of an Annual Conference, the Central Pennsylvania. Sturdy people—those Danes!"

STATUS IS MORE THAN SEX

Built on the solid foundations of the past, the present work of United Methodist women in all phases of

Church life, clergy and lay, has expanded greatly in the past few years, much of the growth occurring since Roy retired in 1972. He says that all this is "logical and past due." He adds:

"As it comes I hope the womanhood of the Church will hold strongly their personal convictions on all matters, and will avoid simply following a party line. I see no reason why a woman should not be a district superintendent or a bishop or hold any other high office in the Church, if she is qualified. I do not believe that any woman should be selected simply on the basis of being a woman, any more than any man should be elected to represent any particular faction or party in the Church or simply because he is a man. If Georgia Harkness were still living, I could enthusiastically cast my vote for her—if I had a vote. The Church ought to recognize stature wherever it is to be found."

Of course Roy has been present in Council meetings, with voice but not vote (since retirement). He has been an intent listener in the frequent discussion on clergy divorces, homosexuality, abortion and other issues arising out of the sexual revolution of our times.

Roy is grateful for the careful work being done by the active bishops on the new problem—and opportunity—of appointing clergy couples. He accepts the fact that there are cases where both man and wife are ready and qualified to serve, and he sees no reason why the appointive system we have cannot handle the situation, given an atmosphere in which the couple and the congregation are willing to cooperate.

THE DECORATIVE HORSE COLLAR

Louise is an inveterate collector of old and new articles, as well as ideas used and unused, from all sorts of places and all kinds of people. "We have to plan for an extra room in the house to store all the stuff she brings in," he says.

SEXISM AND THE STATUS OF WOMEN

"One day she bought an old horse collar, and I asked her, 'What are you going to do with that?' She said, 'I'm going to hang it up.' And I said, 'What are you going to put in it?' Her answer was short and final: 'Your picture.' " Grounds for divorce? Not with them, for they both have long fuses.

By example more than precept, Roy and Louise show a relaxed attitude towards problems that keep the bishops up nights in Council meetings in all Jurisdictions, and at home in committee meetings. The Shorts know the statistics, but they are not horrified or terrified. At a briefing for new bishops, held at Gatlinburg, Tennessee, in 1964, they taught some of the newcomers a few games they had learned years ago. (They may or may not have known that a group of the newly elected had formed a caucus to see what they could do to bring the bishops up-to-date.)

Roy sees the today's Annual Conferences having a most important role to play in preventing the breakdown of clergy families. He holds that retreats for clergy and spouses should be organized for the strengthening and enrichment of marriage and family life. He believes that an appropriate time for such retreats would surely be early in the probation period of the minister.

Although Roy has given primacy in his ministry to preaching, he does not agree with the bishop of another day who said: "I'm up to my ears in counselors, and I would trade four of them for one good preacher any day." Roy contends that wise family counseling is greatly needed by every ministerial family, as well as others. "Every minister, every district superintendent and every bishop should be such a good counselor," he says, and adds:

"I have sought to be a counselor to my children, my friends, my parishoners, my fellow pastors and even, in these late years, to some of my fellow bishops. Whether I have been in any way helpful only the good Lord himself knows."

NOTES—SHORT AND LONG

1. In Southern Methodism the name of the local church unit was "society" and, unlike the practice in the North, there was no division into "foreign" and "home" fields after 1910.
2. With tongue in cheek Louise tells of a visit made to a deaconess motherhouse in Hamburg, Germany, in 1954. In the war-wrecked city the women, who worked for mere subsistence, were doing heroic tasks. She wrote back to friends in Nashville: "My husband fell in love with the deaconesses in Hamburg. He is much interested in their work. I am sure you will hear him speak on that when we return."
3. An evangelistic service in the Cuban canefields was in marked contrast with services in the plush Roman Catholic churches in Havana. People came miles on foot. (Only one in the entire company was on horseback.) In a jeep the missionaries brought the foreign visitors from the barrio, with its thatched roofs. The little church in the fields was jammed with people, swatting flies and singing lustily. After the long service of praying and preaching, they would go back to the fields, to begin work at dawn.

13

ECUMENICITY—BEGINNING WITH US

When he was only a young preacher Roy realized that, like charity, ecumenicity begins at home. (He never did relish the sound of "ecumenics" although he knows that this term deals with problems and strategy, while "ecumenicity" has to do with qualities and feelings.)

From his younger days he was aware that the deep-down needs of Christians cut across the denominational lines, even though individual persons and groups make differing responses. For example, there was a night at the fairgrounds in Columbus, Ohio, when 800 Cadet Corps boys were getting settled down for their first night at the historic Centenary Exposition.

"We were to be there a month, and on that first night I had trouble screwing up my courage to the point where I could kneel beside my cot and say my prayers, so I decided that I would pull the covers over my head and do my praying 'in the privacy of my closet,' as the scriptures have it.

"The second Sunday night at suppertime a boy from Massachusetts stood up and said, 'I would like for any of you boys who will to meet me for a moment after supper. I'd like to say a word to you.'

"None of us had any idea what that word would be. About twenty gathered around him in answer to his request. He took

out his Testament and began to read. It was the verse that says, 'I am not ashamed of the gospel of Christ' (Rom. 1:16). He said:
" 'I had to speak to you fellows tonight. At home, every night before I go to bed, I kneel down beside the bed and say my prayers. But when I came here I was too embarrassed to do it, and I climbed into bed and pulled a sheet over my head and prayed in silence. Now I have to confess it.'
"I said, 'Me, too!' All around the circle the boys said, 'Me, too!' And from that time I knew that Methodists on both sides of the Mason and Dixon Line were very much alike.
"At the Centenary Exposition there were exhibits from all the mission fields, with the Methodists in a special space in the great exhibits hall." Roy was particularly interested in what they had from India, and he kept talking about it. Finally, a boy from Delaware, Ohio, said to him, "Why don't you shut up talking about India? You are a Southern Methodist, and the Southern Methodists don't have any work in India." Roy said, "Sure they do." Let him continue:
"The next day I went around to the India exhibit and found Bishop Francis W. Warne. I asked him whether the Southern Methodist Church had work there and he replied, 'No, son, only the Methodist Episcopal Church.' I went home disappointed because I was not sharing in preaching the gospel in India.
"Twenty years went over my head, and I was a delegate to the Uniting Conference in Kansas City. When union was finally consummated the first thought that came to my mind was, 'I'm preaching in India at last!' "

TWO THOUSAND DEWY-EYED METHODISTS

When Roy talks about Methodist unification (or reunion) at Kansas City in 1939, he becomes lyrical. He was a

ECUMENICITY—BEGINNING
WITH US

delegate there, and he will never forget the moment when Bishops John M. Moore, Edwin Holt Hughes and James H. Straughn stood before the great crowd in the Convention Hall and sealed the union with clasped hands.[1]

At the press table, where Dr. Ralph Stoody presided in those fateful days, there was a reporter for one of the Nashville papers. His name was Percy Priest, later Congressman Priest, for he ran for Congress and was elected. But, at Kansas City, in the month of May, 1939, he was covering this never-before meeting. He said to the reporters:

"You Methodists are going to have to cry a little tomorrow. You'll make a liar of this reporter if you don't, because I have already sent in my story, beginning with the statement that this auditorium was filled with 'dewy-eyed Methodists.' " His prophecy came true, and American Methodism was literally born again at this meeting. The growing-up process was slowed by the complex of problems that came out of Pearl Harbor and the Second World War, but the Church was never the same. (See "Desegregation—by Reconciliation," chapter 16, for an account of what Roy did to use the new Jurisdictional system.)

WORLD METHODISM—CENTRIFUGAL AND
CENTRIPETAL

There was an Ecumenical Conference of Methodists in Atlanta in 1930. Roy and Louise, who were then serving a small church in a Kentucky town, decided to go. They discovered that Methodists of all races and from both sides of the Atlantic could pray together even though they might differ on theology and church structure.

Roy was to value highly his personal opportunities in the World Council of Churches and the National Council of Churches of Christ in the U.S.A., but he gave most of his idea

123

time and thought to the World Methodist Council, which came out of those ten-year Ecumenical Committee meetings that, at first, involved only British and American Methodists.[2] From 1966 to 1972 Roy served on the Executive Committee, which meets in various parts of the Methodist world, and for half of that period he was a vice-president. He had prepared a paper for the meeting at Denver, Colorado, in 1971, but a change in the program schedule prevented him from making the speech. Roy wrote:

"The divisions in Methodism that have marked the passing of the years have grown out of differences over policy, over theological interpretation, over reaction to certain leadership, and over divided opinion on social issues. Again, they have grown out of race and out of national attachment and the desire to be more effective and free in a given national situation." These are the fragmentations due to centrifugal force.

"At the same time that this centrifugal force has operated in Methodism, a companion centripetal force continues to operate today." He mentioned, in describing this drawing together tendency, such agents as Methodist preaching and Methodist testimony, and the fellowship experiences that "probably could be best provided at the regional level."

He thinks of the World Methodist Council as a forum in which Methodists of the world can talk over common problems and concerns, as well as common responses. He put in his paper:

"This is not to reject our participation in ecumenical dialogue, and certainly not to suggest any such thing as some Methodist block position, but it is conceivable that occasion may arise when it may be desirable to be able to voice a general Methodist position or conviction. The World Methodist Council could become more than a forum; it could be a function-serving agency for Methodists everywhere."

There could be such projects as the present worldwide crusade of evangelism. And Roy is grateful for having had the privilege of serving on the committee that met in London and Bermuda under the pioneering leadership of Bishop F. Gerald Ensley and Dr. Alan Walker. In the meetings of worldwide Methodism he met such leaders as Harold Roberts, Eric Baker, Benson Perkins and, more recently, Kenneth Greet.

AGREED, WE WALK TOGETHER

Roy was to have a large part in the union that took place in Dallas in 1968 when the Methodists and Evangelical United Brethren became one Church—The United Methodist Church. In a paper he wrote on prospects and problems, he looked forward to the new opportunity that would come when those who had long been identified in Christian fellowship, a common tradition, a like emphasis on Wesleyan essentials and a similar loyalty to our Lord, as well as a common hope came together, under God, for a new world tomorrow.

Among the bishops Paul A. Washburn, Reuben H. Mueller and Gordon J. Howard carried the heaviest load in the committee on union, as they shared with Methodist Bishops Lloyd Wicke, Gerald Ensley and Roy Short. Roy offers this description:

"In the past such significant changes have come in the life of the Church largely as a result of a ground swell which has gripped the entire Church, or at least a large part of it, over a considerable time. Methodist union in 1939 was the result of such a ground swell. People everywhere wanted union, were talking union, and at last union came. When we approached the possibility of union in 1966 there was no such ground swell. Union had been talked about for years, but there was a lack of information on both sides. We had to accomplish in a short span of years what had taken a much longer time before 1939."[3]

The last Evangelical United Brethren Conference to vote on union met at Naperville, Illinois, and Bishop Harold R. Heininger, who was presiding, asked Roy to preach a series of afternoon sermons on evangelism. Roy says: "The issue was to be decided by the vote in this Conference, and after I returned Bishop Harold Heininger sent me a telegram that the final decision had been made for union."

At the final General Conference of the Evangelical United Brethren Church in Dallas, Bishop Paul A. Washburn was named to be the last in a long line of bishops going back to Philip Otterbein, Martin Boehm and Jacob Albright.[4] Bishop Reuben Mueller was in the chair, and he asked Roy to address the Conference. He was also invited to participate in the consecration of Bishop Washburn.

"It was a great honor and a precious moment," Roy remembers. "I thought of the consecration of Francis Asbury in 1784, with Philip Otterbein present. Bishop Mueller wanted to parallel this historic event. It was surely one of the best hours of my life."

REUNION WITH BLACK METHODISTS

At the 1964 General Conference at Pittsburgh, towering Bishop Sherman Lawrence Greene of the African Methodist Episcopal Church made a strong suggestion that the prevailingly white church should invite the black Methodists to "come home." At Atlanta, in the spring of 1978, there was a joint meeting of 75 bishops, and it was almost as if the invitation to come home were being extended the other way around. There were scholarly papers and much religious enthusiasm with "I hear you, brother!" "Right on!" "Amen and amen!" The altar call for loyalty to the basic realities of our faith was given by eloquent leaders of the black denominations of Methodists.

ECUMENICITY—BEGINNING WITH US

There were four denominations present—the oldest church, United Methodist (1784) with its three daughters: the African Methodist Episcopal (1816), the African Methodist Episcopal Zion (1821) and the Christian Methodist Episcopal (1870). In a hardworking session of 27 hours, the bishops read papers, reacted in plenary meetings and structured discussion groups, debated findings briefly and produced a message. Caucuses and party spirit were at a minimum. The participants were all bishops, and the whole emphasis was on what bishops can do, not only individually but together. Roy was present at the meeting, and while he did not share in the program, he did serve as a behind-the-scenes resource person, and a participant in group discussion.

"We Share a Common Ministry and Episcopacy," was Bishop Philip R. Cousins's theme and he said: "This consultation of Methodist bishops resurrects in me some ambivalent feelings concerning ecumenics and Methodism. I am proud of my Blackness and my Black heritage. Can Blackness and Methodism be one in Christ? Perhaps this consultation will be a step in the right direction, helping to resolve for me, and many others like me, the ambivalence which hinders our being one in Christ."

The paper centered around the history, function and collegiality in our Episcopacy. "As connectional bishops we share the responsibility of the whole Church. The United Methodist Church still holds to this promise even in its Jurisdictional system which elects and assigns bishops. Ours is a sent, or assigned ministry, maintained and persuaded through the appointive power of the bishop."

There was much discussion of theology—like the teaching of Christian perfection, which Bishop Reuben L. Speaks called "the ethical counterpart of the Christian gospel of human liberation."

As Bishop William R. Cannon had been the opening

speaker on "Our Common Doctrine and Discipline," Bishop James K. Mathews led in an unforgettable service of Holy Communion. The message hoped that, just possibly, a step toward union will come with the anniversary of the Christmas Conference in Baltimore in 1984.

ECUMENICITY—BEGINNING WITH US

NOTES—SHORT AND LONG

1. The Methodist Protestant Church, which joined the Methodist Episcopal Church and Methodist Episcopal Church, South, at that meeting, had left the parent church in 1830 because of differences over the episcopacy and lack of lay representation. But Methodist Protestants elected two bishops immediately before the meeting—Bishop James H. Straughn and Bishop John C. Broomfield. Later Bishops Kenneth W. Copeland, Fred Holloway and John B. Warman came out of the Methodist Protestant tradition.
2. Of course, these meetings were not really ecumenical, for they involved only American and British Methodists. But the 10-year meetings led to the World Methodist Council in 1947, and the 5-year meetings after that. Now the combined membership includes some 40 nations and more than 30 million people.
3. The quotation is from a paper that Bishop Short wrote in 1965 for publication in *Together*.
4. Nine Evangelical United Brethren bishops continued in office when their church came into the union. Bishop Washburn was elected by the last Evangelical United Brethren General Conference in 1968 at Dallas. Two bishops with Evangelical United Brethren tradition—Wayne Clymer and Joseph Yeakel—have been elected since 1968.

14

BISHOPS IN POLITICAL CRISES

*L*eaf through the episcopal messages of our Methodist bishops, along with the Evangelical and United Brethren and all other denominations, including the Roman Catholics, and you will conclude that some bishops have always been in politics. So were the prophets of Israel and the holy ones (even today's warring ayatollahs) of Islam. Mahatma Gandhi, orthodox Hindu, whose favorite Christian hymn was "When I Survey the Wondrous Cross," was a consummate politician. Only the Buddhists among the classical religionists have usually been nonpolitical.

Roy Short, careful historian that he is, talks about American Methodists in political crises and begins with Bishop Matthew Simpson, who dabbled in politics while he was president of Indiana Asbury University (later DePauw) and when he was editor of *The Western Christian Advocate* and later when he plunged in deeply at the time his friend Abraham Lincoln took a strong stand on slavery. Roy explains:

"Bishop Simpson was a personal advisor to Presidents Lincoln, Grant, Garfield, Arthur and Hayes. He took a tough lead in the effort to impeach President Andrew Johnson, who succeeded Lincoln.

"The bishop even demanded that post office appointments

BISHOPS IN POLITICAL CRISES

be handed to Methodists in proportion to the percentage of the population that they represented. During the Civil War, along with Bishop Edward R. Ames, he took the position that the conquests of the Union Army should become also the conquests of the Methodist Episcopal Church. He, therefore, urged upon the Secretary of War the filling of Southern Methodist pulpits in occupied territory by Methodist Episcopal ministers.

"Generally, other Methodist Episcopal bishops were active politically at the local and state levels, especially so far as the liquor traffic was concerned. The Anti-Saloon League, largely Methodist in its constituency, and the Methodist Board of Temperance were untiringly active politically, to bring about the passage of the Prohibition Amendment.

"The Southern bishops generally looked with disfavor on political activity, but this pattern was broken by Bishop James Cannon, Jr., who in 1928 led the fight to prevent the election of New York's Al Smith as President. Bishop Cannon was generally credited with the removal, in that year, of several Southern states from the Democratic Party column. A few other Southern bishops joined him, to some extent, in his efforts.

"Since Methodist union in 1939 the bishops have not been reticent to speak out on political issues and to enter political activities of different sorts."

POLITICS—"THEIRS" AND "OURS"

The long revered dogma of the separation of church and state has been pushed into the background in these nation-centered times, but there is still, among our Methodist people, strong opposition against what is termed the "politicization" of our Church. Political activists are having a hard time, even on such issues as the Equal Rights Amendment, which the Council of Bishops endorsed.

The debate, not merely about the propriety but also the effectiveness of Christianity in politics, goes on; and the complexities of political tensions and solutions make it increasingly difficult to separate our American politics from Chinese politics or Russian politics.[1] This confusion raises prickly problems for diplomats and business people, as well as missionaries.

In the late sixties the World Division of the then Board of Missions had this paragraph in its handbook for missionaries:

"We realize that the national churches should enjoy autonomy, and that the missionary responsibility towards countries is primarily theirs. But we also admit the possibility of extreme cases in which the church in the United States feels that, in faithfulness to the Gospel, it must act outside, or even against the will of the national church. The church in the United States must be very careful before embarking in this direction, particularly when the questions have a socio-political nature."

These were carefully weighed words that offered both threat and promise in the self-determination of peoples and of churches trying to serve their own people. To young Asians meeting at a board-sponsored Methodist missionary conference in Kuala Lumpur in 1971 this seemed like "the same old paternalism," but extremists at the meeting changed their slogan from "Missionaries—Go Home!" to something like "Stay—and Work with Us."

The United Board for Christian Higher Education in Asia has kept working away at its innovative programs, breaking through the barriers of the status quo to find new solutions and new meanings. It became increasingly clear that, although competent observers were coming back to the United States with news that "the East is Red," Christian colleges and universities in Asia could play a key role in modifying that fact in the tomorrows.[2] While the Council of Bishops had given no encouragement to Communists in China, the first bishops to make official visits returned with ideas about education—and they looked forward to more than science and technology.[3]

BISHOPS IN POLITICAL OFFICE

"A new phenomenon in recent years," Roy reports, "is represented in the election of two bishops to political office abroad. Bishop Bennie de Quency Warner, of Liberia, has become vice-president of his country. Bishop Abel T. Muzorewa of Zimbabwe-Rhodesia was made prime minister, though he took a leave of absence from his Area while he was leading in the development of a new constitution.

"Bishops of an earlier date would probably have taken the position that a bishop could not retain his episcopal office and, at the same time, accept political office. But the Council has been proud of these two brother bishops, as shown in the fact that the issue of dual responsibility has not been raised. Bishop Warner has continued to carry both responsibilities without any apparent difficulty, and Bishop Muzorewa was released temporarily from episcopal responsibility in order to carry his heavy load as prime minister."[4]

Other bishops are serving in countries where political problems are particularly difficult at present, but where they are giving creative leadership. Bishop Armin Haertel sends heartening reports from the German Democratic Republic (East Germany), Bishop Fama Onema from Zaire, Bishop Emilio de Carvalho from Angola and Bishop Naon Wahadilo from Mozambique.

COMMUNISM HATCHES CRISES

Roy was only a highschooler when Communism, as it is now known, began to claim center stage. He remembers something of the Red scare that gripped the United States during the First World War. From his boyhood memories he reports:

"The first time this registered with me was in 1919 when I served with the Cadet Corps at the Centenary Exposition in Columbus, Ohio. Night after night the rumor went around at the fairgrounds that, out of the nowhere the Communists were about to take over, but just how, or when, or where nobody seemed to know.

"I recall how, in my student days, that I resented the common tendency to dub as Communism any purpose that looked forward or any form of social advance and to identify Socialism with Communism. In my early episcopacy I lived through the period when social prophets were accused of being either outright Communists or dupes of Communism, and when the charge was made that the Church had become badly infiltrated, I joined with my fellow bishops in deep resentment.

"At the same time I realized that Communism is a force to be reckoned with, and to be recognized for what it is and what it does to people. It does destroy freedom in any true sense of the word. It does oppress its satellite countries. I shall never forget the impression of sadness made on my mind and heart on the occasion of my one and only visit to Czechoslovakia. I sensed this atmosphere in other satellite countries to which I have gone, but never to the degree that I felt it there.

"Communism is, of course, the enemy of religion. Where it does tolerate religion to some degree, including the Soviet Union itself, Communism reduces religion to little more than worship rather than attempting to operate as a full-fledged

BISHOPS IN POLITICAL CRISES

religious faith. Without resorting to war it does practice a strategy that, again and again, causes confusion, complication, embarrassment and often extreme difficulties for the non-Communist world. And it has not hesitated to send its armies to take over other countries that have been self-governing for long years when it considered it to its advantage to do so.

"We are not understood as bishops or as a Church when we have too little to say about the wrongs of Communism. And we are still less understood when we give any impression that we are so thrilled with certain gains made by Communist regimes in providing food, employment and health services that we forget the priceless worth of freedom or overlook the fact that humankind connot live by bread alone."

NOTES—SHORT AND LONG

1. In November, 1972, *The Christian Advocate* printed an article entitled, "Can the Missionary Be Involved in Politics?" by Bishop T. Otto Nall, who had recently finished a four-year stint in Hong Kong-Taiwan. He asked such question as these: "Whose politics does the missionary represent? The politics of the people to whom he goes to minister and serve, or the people back home, some of them supporting him with their prayers and money? Does he wear the political labels he had when he came or maybe some new ones? How does he relate the political ideals of his newly found friends and colleagues to world politics in which all of us, as residents and citizens of the whole world, are involved whether we like it or not?"

2. Executive Director Paul T. Lauby, of the United Board for Christian Higher Education in Asia, speaks of the Christian colleges and universities in a letter of September, 1979: "These yeasty academic communities confronted by age-old tradition and rigid government bureaucracies are constantly seeking ways to create intellectual and social ferment, to question basic assumptions, and to point the way to education for human wholeness within a just social order."

3. Soochow University, in Taiwan, has sent 14 professors abroad to complete doctoral degrees in business administration, business mathematics, chemistry, computer science, economics law, mathematics, physics and sociology. They have returned to Taiwan to teach there. Five with masters degrees have returned, too.

4. Bishop Muzorewa's book *Rise Up and Walk* was distributed to the Council, and when Bishop Roy C. Nichols had read it he said: "The beleaguered bishop of Zimbabwe, who is trying desperately to bring peace to his nation, speaks of his early struggle to find a comprehensive theology to embrace the deep and present needs of a people laboring against the

insistent domination of an unrelenting oppressor. He realized, finally, like Moses and the prophets, like Jesus and Paul and all the saints, that God's delivering power and purpose are total, encompassing the soul, body, mind and social experience of the whole family of human personalities."

15
WALKING WITH THE GREAT AND NEAR GREAT

W. M. Bunts was his name—and Roy tells about him: "He was a rugged old preacher in the Holston Conference. He never went too far in school, and he was awkward in manner, but I have known few men more effective in helping young people. He always did what he did for them by the process of buttonholing and personal contact.

"Years ago there was a ministerial candidate at Emory and Henry College whom everyone called 'Shorty.' He was not too good as a student, and one year at exam time he had failed several of his courses. He was sitting on a rock on the campus, looking blue and dejected when along came Brother Bunts, who asked what the trouble was.

"The lad replied, 'I'll never make it. I have failed again. I just don't have what the other boys have.' And Brother Bunts said, 'I'll tell you what, Shorty, if you can't be smart, you can be good. You major in goodness and get top grades in that, and you'll come out all right.'

"The lad took the advice and decided to do just that, and if I have known any men and women who have succeeded in majoring in goodness, he is among those who take front rank in that company."

For Roy greatness has been about nine-tenths goodness, and he checked out the big-name people for their sincerity, integrity and devotion, all qualities of what he would call "goodness." He says:

"In later years, emphasis on personal religion has not been as strong amongst us as some of us might wish. Other concerns—entirely proper concerns—have sometimes occupied our attention almost exclusively. And then, too, some of us have feared that too strong emphasis on personal religion might lead—as it undoubtedly has at times—to overlooking or neglecting the social aspects of religion. Again, some of us, in reacting against a pietism that could not command our full respect have been tempted to identify all personal religion with such pietism, for we know that genuine religion can have about it nothing artifical."

WHEN A BOY LOOKS AT A PRESIDENT

"The first President of the United States I ever saw was Woodrow Wilson," Roy remembers. "As a Boy Scout I went to Hodgenville, Kentucky, in 1916, for the dedication of the Lincoln Memorial. We Scouts formed a line up the steps of the memorial building, and the tall, scholarly man from Columbia, South Carolina, by way of Princeton passed within a dozen yards of me.

"I got a glimpse of Calvin Coolidge in 1925 when I visited the White House for the first time. I heard Herbert Hoover speak at Louisville during the 1928 presidential campaign. After I became a bishop I met Presidents Eisenhower, Kennedy, Johnson, Nixon and Carter for the first time. Of course, I have been impressed by the position they have occupied, and in some of them I have detected qualities of leadership that I thought explained why they were elected. But I have been no more impressed by such chief executives than by some of the church heroes I have known.

"As a boy I found the Church as my life, and I missed no

opportunity to see and hear as many bishops as I could. The first bishop I heard preach was John Carlisle Kilgo, once president of Trinity College which became the present Duke University. In my boyhood I listened with rapt attention to Bishops Elijah E. Hoss, Henry Clay Morrison and James Atkins, all gone now for more than half a century. As a lad I heard all the bishops who, during those years, held the Louisville Conference, including Bishops Denny, Darlington, Dickey, Candler, McMurry, DuBose and Watkins. With one exception all of them were strong and moving preachers."

Roy became an avid reader of episcopal biographies. And when, a few years ago in a devotional given at the Council of Bishops meeting, he picked out the voices that seemed to speak something important for the day in which we live, he went far back to name four voices long since stilled.

Bishop Isaac W. Joyce, who felt inferior in episcopal company in comparison with more gifted brethren, said: "God gives me something too—he gives me access to souls." Another voice was Bishop Thomas Bowman, who was known as "the children's bishop because he was their friend and champion." Another was Bishop Robert McIntyre, a bricklayer by trade, dubbed "Il Pensoroso" by his colleagues because he was usually lost in thought, who became a giant of a preacher. And the fourth was Bishop John C. Granbery, a good man who served for years as a Vanderbilt professor. When the General Conference of 1882 was approaching, Bishop McIntyre said of him, "The Church is not thinking now of Granbery, but when it gets to praying, it will remember him."[1]

PREACHERS ARE THE GREATEST

Roy makes no apologies for putting preaching in first place among the excellencies of the ministry, and he comes back, time and time again, to the standards that Dr. John A. Broadus set for a good sermon: it must convince the judgment; it must touch the emotions; it must call forth a response of the will.

The evangelistic preachers thrilled Roy. He remembers the camp-meeting greats that he heard when he went with his mother: Bud Robinson, C. W. Ruth, Will Huff, H. C. Morrison, George R. Stewart, Sam Small, Walt Whitcomb and Luther Bridges. He reflects:

"During seminary days I listened and was lifted when Toyohiko Kagawa, Martin Niemöller, Albert Schweitzer, Merton S. Rice, Frederick Shannon, S. D. Gordon, John Roach Stratton and Newell Dwight Hillis came to the seminary chapel or to old downtown Trinity Church. I noticed that most of them were biblical preachers, and that squared with what I was being taught at the Presbyterian seminary.

"Before seminary, and during my last year in college, I attended the Student Volunteer Convention in Indianapolis in 1924, and there I heard John R. Mott, Sherwood Eddy, Robert E. Speer, Robert Wilder and others who were speaking to the minds and, particularly, the hearts of the younger generation of that day."

ULYSSES AMONG EVANGELISTS—A LAYMAN

"Actually, I did not see Dr. Mott again, until twenty-four years later, in 1948, when I was a bishop in Florida. He was far along in years then. He was in the audience at First Church, Orlando, one morning when I was preaching. I noticed that he wrote all the time, and it disturbed me, for I thought that I had lost his attention entirely. I perhaps was not saying anything worth his listening to. Later I learned that he had made a lifelong habit of taking notes of every sermon or address he heard. Dr. John Branscomb introduced me to him, and he wrote me a letter when he reached home and sent me a full set of his writings.

"One day not long after Dr. Mott died, I had lunch in Singapore with D.T. Niles. In the course of the table conversation Dr. Niles said, 'Did you ever hear about Mott's last visit to the World Council of Churches?' (The reference was to the Central Committee, of which I later became a member.) I said I had not, and he told me about it.

"He said that this was when the famed preaching layman was up in years, and not his old self. As a privileged character he would wander in and out of meetings. Finally, he came in for what proved to be his last time. As he left the room, he turned to the group and said,'When John Mott is dead, remember that he was an evangelist.' "

Roy recalls that Billy Sunday and Gypsy Smith both came to Louisville when he was a young preacher in the first years of ministry. A big tabernacle was erected, and each preacher stayed about a month. Roy was there every night. He comments:

"The two evangelists were in striking contrast in both their messages and manner of presentation. One was an apostle of judgment, and the other an apostle of love. The music in the Billy Sunday meeting was in charge of the great choir leader and trombonist Homer A. Rodeheaver. Little did I realize that, in less than thirty years, he and I would be working together in revivals at Daytona Beach, Orlando, and St. Petersburg. He was not only a capable song leader, but a pleasant and inspiring companion. An hour spent with him and some others in a home after the services was relaxation indeed."[2]

Since Roy attended all the religious meetings he could, he heard the preachings of E. Stanley Jones, W. E. Sangster, Forney Hutchinson, James R. Gray, Edwin Lewis, Henry Hitt Crane, Ralph Sockman, Ralph Diffendorfer, Harold

WALKING WITH THE GREAT
AND NEAR GREAT

Bosley, Clovis Chappell, Charles R. Goff, Roy Smith, Ernest F. Tittle and Nels Ferré. Among the women preachers he heard were: Daisy Davies, Evangeline Booth, Georgia Harkness and Estelle Carver.

He tells about Amy Semple McPherson and her preaching in Angelus Temple, Los Angeles. "With the spotlight thrown on her she came down a long ramp in a flowing white robe, and she carried a bouquet of red roses, which she proceeded to toss to the audience. She preached on the text, 'They cast four anchors out of the stern, and wished for the day' (Acts 27:29)." Roy says: "As I saw her coming down that ramp I thought that a Methodist preacher walking quietly into his pulpit in his cutaway coat and striped pants did not really have a chance."[3]

DISCIPLE—AND PRINCE OF PREACHERS

Roy has this to say about the famed George Truett of Dallas:

"I think that I never tried to copy any one preacher, although I studied every one I heard and learned what I could from each. I did not attempt to analyze whether they were biblical, topical, allegorical or whatever kind of preachers—I merely wanted to see what styles were most effective.

"The great Truett I heard twice—once on the road and once in his Dallas pulpit. I shall never forget that first time. His serious and intent expression impressed me. I shall always remember what he said: 'If I had a thousand lives, let them all preach Christ to the end of every day.' I was young then—I wonder what impression those of us who are preaching today make upon the younger generation. We shall not know until today's youth live to middle age."

Roy remembers too the preacher-teacher Rollin H. Walker, who molded the thinking of generations of students at Ohio

Wesleyan. In a conversation with him in a Mobile, Alabama, motel Roy asked him why we today do not seem to have the unique preachers, teachers and lawyers of other days. Dr. Walker replied: "The era of the self-made man or woman is largely gone. We are turning out students who are machine products rather than handmade. Few people now are self-taught."

Roy had a high appreciation for the preachers in his own Louisville Conference, and especially the 11 young men who were admitted to that Conference with him in 1921. Only three of that class remain as this is written—J. W. Rayburn, W. H. Russell and Roy Short.[4] He says: "They may not have Annual Conferences in Heaven, but a lot of the company I have loved have gone on to that blessed country, and I often find myself thinking of the Louisville Conference 'on the other side.'"

NOTES—SHORT AND LONG

1. This material is from Bishop Short's address to the Council of Bishops in New Orleans in November, 1975. The title: "Some Voices We Hear."
2. Bishop Short took an active part in many evangelistic campaigns over the years. He was chairman of a Billy Graham compaign in Louisville. Of course, he did not share the criticism of the evangelist voiced by some in the 1972 General Conference.
3. When preacher-editor Roy L. Smith was asked why he muted his dramatic methods (he had been a Chautauqua floor manager) when he moved from Minneapolis to Los Angeles, he said: "Amy Semple McPherson was so much better than I that I did not want my hearers to make comparisons."
4. An interesting statistic: From the Annual Conferences where he has presided as bishop, Roy Short has seen these ministers elected to the episcopacy: Bishop Branscomb (1952), Bishop Hodge (1956), Bishop Henley (1960), Bishop Hunt (1964) and Bishop Tullis (1972). He was also in the Area in which Bishops Pendergrass, Stokes, Blackburn and Armstrong served as ministers, but not at the time of their election. He was present at the Southeast Asia Conference when Bishop Robert Lundy, who was a product of the Holston Conference, was elected.

16

DESEGREGATION—BY RECONCILIATION

*R*oy Short did not use this story, which he knows well, when he spoke to the Northeastern Jurisdictional Conference in June, 1964, but it would have fitted in.

It happened that a social worker was coaching her girls in a Lower East Side settlement house to do their parts in a biblical drama about the virgins who took oil and those who did not to the wedding feast at Cana.[1] They insisted on saying "url" for "oil." Finally, in desperation, the teacher took one girl to the window and pointed to a bird sitting on the limb of a tree. "Look," she said, "that is a 'bird,' not a 'boid.' " To which the obstinate student replied, "Well, it choips like a boid."

Everything went well the night the pageant was presented. The lines were said accurately until the time for the little girl to speak of the virgins who took no oil. In her nervousness "oil" came out "url." The mother was heartbroken by her daughter's mistake after all the coaching. "Oh," she said, "she spurled it!"

Roy began by pointing out that Methodism has continually divided on more important matters than pronunciation, and he underscored the function of the Jurisdictional plan, or system, in recognizing differences. "These differences are not always major, but they do have significance," he said. Loyal

DESEGREGATION—BY RECONCILIATION

Methodists can no more divorce themselves from the total context in which their day-by-day lives are lived than can other people. New England is not South Georgia, and urban New York is considerably different from Ozark country in Arkansas and Missouri.

"All of us are more or less affected by the problems, the mores, the ways of thinking, the traditions and the patterns of life in that part of the world that we call home. For either liberal or conservative to deny this is to fail to be objective. These local factors should not be finally determinative for us, but to acknowledge their existence is only being realistic. This the Jurisdictional system does."

He went on to talk about the protection that the Jurisdictional plan of Methodist Church government, which is essentially regional, affords to minorities. "In a Church the size of Methodism every part of the Church is necessarily a minority," he said. "The genius of the Jurisdictional system is its provision against any part of the Church becoming a helpless minority. The plan provides this first of all by balancing among the Jurisdictions representation upon the various boards and agencies of the Church,[2] and by the election of bishops in the Jurisdictional Conferences. . . . Whether the Jurisdictional system results in the election of an episcopacy whose members are as widely known as might be wished may well be open to question. It is not open to debate, however, that it does result in a more distributed episcopacy and one in better position to be more knowledgeable of the Church at local levels."

Roy recognized that, at the time he spoke—and the situation is now changed—the Central Jurisdiction was a constitutional symbol of racial segregation. While he pointed out some ways in which the Central Jurisdiction had been of advantage to the Blacks, he went on to discuss the advantages that the system brings to "Conferences finding themselves with the same concerns and, in the case of geographic Jurisdictions, in contiguous territory and associated together, as the Southeastern and South Central Jurisdictions are, for administrative purposes." He mentioned missions, evangelism, social concerns, education and lay work.

DRIVING WITH A REIN NOT TOO TIGHT

"From the beginning, three of the Jurisdictions of the Church have chosen to make little use of the Jurisdictional system," Roy explained. "The northern and western parts of the Church, in the interest of a larger union, took due account of the fear of an all-powerful General Conference long obtaining in other sections of the Church, and went along with the checks and balances afforded by the Jurisdictional system, but so far as they were concerned, let the Jurisdictional system remain as simply that and nothing more. After all, in these sections of the Church the Area system was working well."

He added: "Another reason for the lack of enthusiasm for the Jurisdictional system in some parts of the Church has been the absence of institutions jointly owned or operated by all the Conferences of the Jurisdiction. There was a degree of arbitrariness in constituting the geographical Jurisdiction," and he illustrated by mentioning New England and West Virginia in the Northeastern Jurisdiction, Ohio and the Dakotas in the North Central. "This was done largely in the interest of achieving numerical and geographical balance."

He warned against fragmentation of the Church through abuse of the Jurisdictional system and suggested that we might learn some lessons from the congregational type of churches and from other Methodist bodies such as the British Methodists who know "something of the practical wisdom of driving with a rein that is not too tight."

He predicted: "With both its possible advantages and its possible handicaps, we probably have the Jurisdictional system, with the exception of the Central Jurisdiction, with us for some time to come."

INTEGRATION OF CONFERENCES—NOW OR WHEN?

Two years later, when Roy spoke with other Southeastern Jurisdictional bishops, much water had gone over the dam—much of it dirty water. He said: "The Methodist Church in the Southeast, and to some extent the South Central states, faces the most serious situation it has been called to face since the first General Conference following the close of the Civil War. That was in New Orleans, and the time was 1866, exactly one hundred years ago."

He called the roll of episcopal leaders then—McTyeire, Marvin, Doggett, Wightman and others who were determined to find a way through. "It is to be hoped that some, at least partially comparable leadership may emerge to match itself against the problems of this our day in our section of the land. At present Methodist unity is badly broken and, at points, Methodist union is under severe strain.

"The mood of cordial, mutual acceptance that characterized us in the beginning days is now almost totally gone. . . . Old North-South antagonisms have been strongly revived in the Church as elsewhere.

"There is now a marked impatience with us in the South on the part of much of the remainder of the Church. Some of this may be unjustified, but for much of it we Southerners must assume some measure of responsibility. It is only to be expected that some things that have happened in our own churches in recent years should produce a reaction of shock, indignation and anger."

He referred to three Judicial Council decisions,[3] as well as actions by such groups as Methodists for Church Renewal. He reported that there was strong pressure for desegregation of Annual Conferences everywhere and a disposition to make this a condition of union with the Evangelical United Brethren Church.[4] He said: "It appears now that there will be efforts at the special General Conference at Chicago in 1966 to amend the Evangelical United Brethren plan of union to force the immediate integration of Conferences and perhaps other strong steps that could mean a shifting of the debate to the race issue and away from the union itself.

"Many of us feel that it is not fair to make the Evangelical United Brethren union with us carry the burden of whatever adjustments the Methodist Church should be making in the field of race. Nothing could possibly be gained racially except to move action forward by one or two years, which under our normal Methodist schedule we could not be considering until 1968. To run the risk of the defeat of union for the sake of so brief a time span hardly seems either wise or fair."

Roy suggested a paper from the Southeastern bishops including a clear declaration of each one's personal position as a bishop on the race issue; a joint statement, with supporting data, on the state of opinion in the Southeastern Jurisdiction; an insistance on the pastoral rather than the legal approach in solving the race problem; a careful assessment of what the bishops believed will happen in an inclusive Church if every point is forced; some honest, positive statement of what the bishops think can be done, with attention to varying conditions from state to state; some forthright statement of what Conference mergers will do on the border and in the deeper South; a statement of the willingness of the bishops to assume pastoral responsibility; some prediction of what can be done about transfer of ministers and, in 1968, the placing of at least one Black bishop in each Jurisdiction; other suggestions for unity of leadership in approaching such crucial matters.

DESEGREGATION—BY
RECONCILIATION

Much was made of the 1967 deadline for completing preparations for the end of the Central Jurisdiction in 1968.

NOW, SPEAKING OF KENTUCKY—

Although there had been friendly relationships between black and white Methodist churches in Kentucky for a long, long time, merger was not too easy when the time came. In 1961 and again in 1962, both the Louisville Conference and the Kentucky Conference took action, without urging, to effect a merger of Conferences, but the offers were not accepted by the Tennessee-Kentucky Conference. Again, in 1967, when Conferences across the Church were voting on merger, the Tennessee-Kentucky Conference refused, almost unanimously.

Roy wrote in 1970:

"Our white people in Kentucky—particularly our liberal leadership—were greatly disappointed. They had felt that, if merger could not be worked out in Kentucky, it could not be worked out in other Areas where the problems were obviously more complex. Therefore, we were delighted when the Tennessee-Kentucky Conference changed its mind, and we could make plans for the merger, which came in 1968.

"There was great jubilation on the days when the Louisville Conference met at Buechel and the Kentucky Conference at the university in Morehead. There black and white Methodists were staying together, newly associated, on the campus. There was continuing opportunity to be together—and they made up for lost time.

"The Evangelical United Brethren churches were also included in these merger sessions, adding further joy to the occasion."

Roy offers some other signs of progress:

"Our black members are taking their places on boards and

agencies of the two Conferences. The vice-president of the Program Council in the Louisville Conference is a Black, as is the lay leader of the Lexington District. The president of the Women's Society in the Kentucky Conference is a Black.

"Our institutions are all integrated, and in some cases this integration antedates merger. This means four hospitals, two in each Conference, and three colleges. And one of the finest examples of integration is our Methodist Home, where there are a number of black children.

"Some of our congregations have been standoffish and have not been as active in seeking Blacks as they should be, but the attendance of some Blacks at services is common all over the Conferences. As the Blacks have told me, they are as eager to keep their local church identity as are white churches. They welcome white visitors and would not bar white persons from joining their fellowship, but they have deeply rooted ties, common attachments and concerns, strong sentiment that makes them hesitate at local church merger.

"One of my chief concerns was to find a place of major responsibility on the level of the whole Louisville Area where I could use some Black minister. The person I had in mind was Dr. Horace H. Greene, and he is now director of Church and Community Planning, directly related to the bishop's office and not the Conference program councils. He goes to New York three times a year to meet with the Bishops' Linkage Group, sponsored by the National Division, Board of Global Ministries. Of course, he meets regularly with our joint cabinet whenever it is in session, on program matters.

"Dr. Greene has been particularly helpful in trying to bring order out of our currently disjointed work in Appalachia." (Roy was writing in 1970.) "His helpfulness to Red Bird Mission has been most appreciated, as have been his contacts with inner-city ministries, rural ministries and involvement with various *ad hoc* groups seeking the support of the Church.

DESEGREGATION—BY RECONCILIATION

"There have been some fears that integration might mean nothing more than absorption. Such fears are unfair, especially to the liberals who have fought valiantly and sacrificially oftentimes to bring a formerly segregated Church to what they judged to be a more Christian inclusiveness."

He pointed out that differences in conditions in various Areas presented varying problems and possibilities. He found himself especially gratified for what happened in South Carolina under the leadership of Bishop Paul Hardin and after that under Bishop Edward L. Tullis.

NOTES—SHORT AND LONG

1. The social worker in this case was Frances Smith, later wife of Dr. Rockwell C. Smith of the Garrett-Evangelical Seminary faculty.

2. Since 1968 a large amount of time has been given in the Jurisdictional Colleges of Bishops to making nominations to boards and commissions and other agencies in accordance with the requirements of the *Discipline*. Careful attention must be given to quotas: the Church depends on the bishops who know their people as no other leaders do.

3. The Judicial decisions referred to concerned: (1) the Jurisdiction giving advice to the Annual Conferences, about boundaries, (2) Annual Conferences proceeding to merge without consulting the Jurisdictional body and (3) identity of the Annual Conference as a constitutional matter.

4. It will be recalled that Bishop Short was one of the episcopal members, from the Methodist side, on the Commission on Union.

17

AREN'T WE ALL MINORITIES?

"Word talk" is the phrase Roy uses for much of the rhetoric about minorities, and that sends us to dictionaries, encyclopedias and such. *The New Columbia Encyclopedia* says that religious minorities were known from ancient times, but ethnic minorities became an issue in European politics with the rise of nationalism in the 19th century. The potential conflict arose from nationalism's equating the nation with the dominant cultural group.

He states that for United Methodists the process began as a feature of what is generally termed the Black revolution. Other groups, seeing the effects of some Black protest, have in turn begun to make their own demands. Chief among these are the Spanish-American group, the Indians and the Orientals.[1]

He adds: "It is now popular jargon to speak of women and youth as minority groups, and often they choose thus to designate themselves. But this is largely word talk. Certainly their situation does not parallel that of the ethnic and racial minorities. While they may not have enjoyed in the past all the privileges which they might desire, and should have had, certainly they have not been deliberately and consciously discriminated against in late years, nor have they known anything approximating segregation or needlessly cruel abuse.

"Now other minorities are also making their appearance in the Church—minorities not based upon race or national origin or age or sex, but minorities coalescing around the theological or social concepts. These, too, are perfecting organizations, holding conferences, and caucuses, resorting to political strategies—and demanding to be heard."

Historian that he is, Roy remembers the union of Methodists in 1939 to make one great inclusive Church, willing to give itself in mission to minorities in the United States and around the world. It organized Annual Conferences among Blacks, Latins, Orientals, Germans, Scandinavians and Indians in the United States and in some forty countries. The device of setting up minority Conferences was not intended to hamper any of these minorities, but to meet their needs and to consolidate their strength. But he warned, back there before the 1972 General Conference, that United Methodism "cannot reasonably expect to stumble into adequate solutions of the problems represented by the current minority picture."

DETERMINING WHAT THE MINORITIES WANT

It is easy to get off the track by concentrating upon the form in which some minority demands are made rather than upon the demands—they are more than requests —themselves, and their relationship to other minority demands in an inclusive Church. In an evangelistic address on "Comprehensive Christianity"[2] Bishop Roy C. Nichols pointed out that, with 79 per cent of United States immigration coming from Africa, Latin America and Asia, "America's color spectrum is deepening. . . . Beyond the year 2000, at present growth rates, approximately one third of the

AREN'T WE ALL MINORITIES?

American people will be non-white." He explains what this means for evangelism:

"The practical requirements of America's international diplomacy is forcing liberalization of immigration policies, in order to cultivate a positive rapport with nations of the Third World, who heretofore were kept under rigid restrictions. It follows, therefore, that a principal church growth opportunity lies in this emerging pigmented section of the population.

"Furthermore, the importance of the African American sector of American Christianity must not be taken for granted. This constituency constitutes 20 per cent of United States Protestantism."

The point at which minorities of all kinds are generally agreed on what they want is greater representation in the General Conference, our chief policy making body. Roy Short says: "So far as ethnic or racial Conferences still remain, this representation is guaranteed. Reports of the election of delegates to the 1972 General Conference indicate that many Conferences have tried to be fully fair, and in some cases, more than fair upon a numerical basis, so far as black delegates are concerned.

"The possibility of more youth delegates waits upon certain changes in the law which will surely come shortly. Once this change is made, youth, like women, must be willing to take their chance on election along with all other United Methodists."

The other place at which the ethnic and racial minorities want more adequate representation is on the boards and agencies of the Church. Minorities want staff members on boards and commissions. As Roy says, "The question remains as to whether such staff representation is to be essentially symbolic or truly functional, and whether it is to be beamed at serving a particular minority group or at the total mission of the total Church."

A number of minority groups appear to be interested in the election of bishops from their number. This is readily understood in the case of the black minority, for the Methodist Church has had Black bishops for more than 50 years, and they will continue to be elected, despite the absence of the old Central Jurisdictional power base.

In the cases of the Spanish-speaking Americans and Indians it is not clear whether these minorities want primarily symbolic representation, or representation for the purpose of administering ethnic units by persons of the same origin. With the Mexicans in the West and the Puerto Ricans in the East and other Spanish units scattered elsewhere it is hard to see how a Spanish-speaking unit could be established that would be workable.

The administration of such a Church as ours is full of tough questions. Not the least of these is how to deal with the desire of some minorities to receive United Methodist funds for independent projects of their own creation or operation—and subject to their own accounting. To make such grants would be a departure from our normal administrative pattern of accountability to our boards and agencies.

A PROBLEM FOR HISTORY

Is the merger of what were formerly ethnic districts and Conferences (German, Scandinavian, Oriental in California, Latin in Florida) working out? Or, are there certain values in separateness—not a separateness that is forced from without, but a separation that is desired and approved by the minority itself? Roy has some more questions:

"Who speaks for a minority? Should the Church have one policy in dealing with a minority of 10,000 and another for a

AREN'T WE ALL MINORITIES?

minority of 300,000? How does a minority leader get his leadership? What about the caucuses and *ad hoc* groups that are largely self-appointed? Should the Church yield to the cry of 'you don't trust us'? What about minorities who have difficulty in finding voice like the rural poor in the United States?"[3]

Roy has other questions that he thinks it his duty to ask, although some have been answered by recent insights of the minority groups themselves:

"Are there minorities which are not racial or ethnic in origin but are to be reckoned with by a Church that is alert to its responsibility for serving God and his children? What about the Methodists for Evangelical Christianity? The probability is that in their basic thinking they represent a far larger minority than any other identifiable minority in the Church. Clearly, the way to deal with them is not to ignore them. There are extremely sad chapters in Methodist history of the yesterdays of inability to deal constructively with so-called evangelical minorities.

"What is the pattern of dealing with such a minority? Also, what about minorities from abroad, since we are still, despite recent autonomous Church developments, to some extent a world Church?"

THE RICHNESS OF OUR DIVERSITY

Roy tells of one of the bishops of thirty years ago who did not conform to type as a bishop, and who used to explain his election to the episcopacy by saying, "The rougher element in the Church rose up and demanded recognition." There are times when the game gets rough and tough and it is hard to live up to the ideal that Roy sets in the words, "We must determine, as a Church, exactly what it is that the minorities want, and what it is that, not 'they' but 'we' deserve and should have, by all standards of justice and Christian love." Assuming that minorities in the Church can and will reach up to the ideal of thinking of the general good ("common welfare" in the language of the American Declaration of Independence) what are the specifics? Prior to the General Conference of 1972, Roy asked such questions as these, and he lists them:

"If a Spanish-speaking bishop is to serve Spanish-speaking people, how is he to be given an Area, with Spanish work scattered in five Jurisdictions? Would there be wisdom in setting up Spanish missionary Conferences around New York, Miami, and perhaps Chicago, and then passing an enabling act to allow, say the South Central Jurisdiction to elect a Spanish-speaking bishop, and have the various colleges of bishops to request him to hold Spanish-speaking Conferences?"

The request for the election of an Indian bishop raises another question. There is only one Indian Conference, and it is small. If the suggestion is that a bishop who is an Indian be elected for assignment to any Area in the electing Jurisdiction, that is one thing. But if he be elected for Indian work, this raises the whole question of the justifiable size for Episcopal Areas.

Roy said directly to the bishops: "We cannot leave the responsibility for coming to grips with these problems with the Board of Missions or some General Conference committee. As those who have responsibility for the general oversight of the Church we, ourselves, need to formulate some definite ideas of our own on this matter."

The Council of Bishops, speaking more formally in the Midquadrennial message, in March, 1978, put it this way:

"The United Methodist Church acknowledges that, to be a Church at all, it must be inclusive. We confess, even in this very year—the 10th since the assassination of Martin Luther

AREN'T WE ALL MINORITIES?

King, Jr.—how often and how sorely we have fallen short of our unique situation among Protestant churches in the United States, gifted as we are with a very sizeable presence among our constituents of Black, Hispanic and Native American peoples as well as persons of Asian ancestry. We welcome the richness of our diversity and encourage the development of the integrity of each part of our varied heritage. We are also mindful of, and grateful for the wide diversity of peoples who make up our congregations of countries outside the United States. In all places we are required to be engaged in ministries of reconciliation in aggressive and affirmative ways."

NOTES—SHORT AND LONG

1. The quotations are from a paper Bishop Short wrote on, "Dealing with Minorities Administratively." It was presented at the Council of Bishops meeting in Des Moines, Iowa, in November, 1971.
2. Bishop Nichols' statement was the keynote address at the Congress of Evangelism in Pittsburgh, January, 1979; his statistics from *U.S. News and World Report,* February 20, 1970.
3. The mission Conferences are Alaska, Oklahoma-Indian, Puerto Rico and Rio Grande as regular Conferences in sections of the United States where Latins are surely not a minority.

18

THE BISHOPS' CHANGING ROLE IN A CHANGING CHURCH

$\mathcal{S}$omewhere up north, it may have been in one of Ohio's industrial towns, Roy picked up the fetching story about the man, always attired in working clothes, who came to the jewelry store every morning about 10 o'clock. He did not go in, but he paused before the window and stared.

The jeweler became curious, even suspicious. He checked with his assistant, who had also watched the man. "Maybe he's trying to find a way to break in," the clerk said. "I don't think so," the owner replied. "Jewelry thieves don't operate that way."

After some two weeks of the same experience, the owner went out. "Good morning, sir," he said. "I notice you coming every morning and admiring something in my window. If there's some article you want for your wife or daughter or somebody, maybe we could make an arrangement. But, why do you come every day at the same time?"

"Oh, I don't want to buy anything. But, I blow the whistle at the factory up there on the hill. My watch must be exactly right, and I know you must keep that fine clock in the window on time, perhaps by electricity. When I blow the whistle the workers start their tasks in the morning, and when I blow again in the afternoon, they go home. So I set my watch by your clock."

The jeweler laughed. "We appreciate the compliment, but we set our clock by your whistle."

And so it is with the United Methodist Church and the bishops: the episcopal leaders try to find out what the Church thinks and how the Church feels, and the Church wonders why the bishops do not tell them.

POWERFUL PENGUINS, THEY ARE

Whoever it was who looked up to the platform at General Conference and saw the bishops sitting quietly, solemnly and more or less contentedly and called them "penguins," the unflattering picture has prompted much good-natured banter. Those shortlegged, flightless birds of the cold waters of Antarctica seem to specialize in being spectators, and so do the voiceless and voteless bishops at General Conference. But they are far from powerless. Their problem is to use the power the Church has given them for the good of the Church.

There has been much talk about current efforts to chip away at the power of the bishops by shortening the period of active service by shifting bishops from Area to Area so that they would not be tempted to identify with the people and settle in. Once in a blue moon—or oftener—a bishop has been accused of trying to dominate a council, board or committee because of his special interest in a pet cause or project. The appointive system, which takes a good deal of a bishop's time (including prayer time) and energy, is overlaid with requirements that are expected to limit the bishop's administrative power when everybody knows—or should know—that he has no real power except what he earns by proper use of his God-given gifts and graces. Could any responsible leader ask for more?

Roy Short has said much, and written even more, about the

THE BISHOPS' CHANGING ROLE IN A CHANGING CHURCH

episcopacy as the Church's responsibility for the churches; that is, Methodism in general giving its life for local Methodism. The aphorism, often attributed to the late Gilbert K. Chesterton, British author and wit and prince of paradoxes, "Nothing ever happens until it happens locally," speaks for the Church, and not only his own church, the Roman Catholic. Roy knows this from his close association with Methodist local churches, small, middle-sized and larger.[1]

There is no "mystique of the episcopacy," or secret skill shared only by the initiated, that marks the bishops as they try to see that we have a mobile ministry, recruited, trained and deployed for congregations of all sizes, colors and dispositions in the United Methodist fellowship. This is the only reason that bishops have any power at all, and they know that the task would be impossible without the qualities of leadership that flow from their own examples of living and experiencing, of believing and listening and proclaiming.

The Council of Bishops is surely the most visible arm of the Church. It has some qualities and duties of its own, a few powers to match its responsibilities for the spiritual and temporal health of the Church; but it is made up only of those persons, men and, hopefully, women, whom the Jurisdictional Conferences send to it. Unquestionably the Council changes them, and they change the Council of Bishops.[2]

"HOW I HAVE SEEN THE BISHOPS CHANGE"

As a superintendent, district and general, here is the way Roy assesses the changes that have come in more than three decades:

"There has been a decided increase in the number of favorite sons elected to the episcopacy. When I was elected in 1948 a number of the bishops had been churchwide figures— denominational executives, editors or sponsors of causes that had attracted national attention. The years have witnessed some churchwide leaders coming into the Council, but most have been of more restricted prominence, chiefly pastors, some of them well known regionally but not nationally known.

"The election of favorite sons is perhaps a natural result of the Jurisdictional plan or system. This promises to be more common under new plans for announcing the nomination of candidates from the Annual Conferences.

"Second, there is a tendency on the part of the average bishop to concentrate his energies and attention more and more on Area rather than general church affairs. (Time was when a different bishop was assigned every year to hold a given Annual Conference and at one period in the earlier years even the General Minutes did not indicate which bishop had the assignment.) The attention to Conference and Area matters has resulted in a pastoral type of episcopacy, not existing in an earlier time.

"Third, there is more informality among the bishops than there once was. The Southern bishops, coming into the Council with Methodist union in 1939, found it hard to pick up the use of first names; and I, for one, find this still a problem, except in the cases of some bishops whom I have known intimately.[3] In later years another informality has developed among the bishops and their wives (matching, perhaps, a custom of public figures on television) of giving a peck on the cheek when meeting. The Council as I first knew it would have been flabbergasted by this. A few of us older ones have not yet mastered the art—or is it a science?

"Fourth, there is disregard for some traditions of the Council that is quite new and strange to some of us. Far less attention is paid to seniority that was once true. Also, an old and honored custom in the Council was that new bishops should be seen and not heard during their first few years. This tradition began to be ignored in the sixties and now most newly elected bishops speak their minds whenever they choose. Despite the continued tradition against a time limit for speeches and the habit of calling for the previous question to close debate, the times when long and irrelevant speeches block the program are now rare. Young and old feel free to participate in town-meeting fashion.

"Fifth, there are fewer dominating figures in the Council than there were 30 years ago, and in the Council itself there is a more general distribution of leadership on committees. More members of the body take part in discussion and debate.

"Sixth, the bishops now travel more extensively than before. At each meeting there are two or three or more who send regrets because they are abroad on official business.[4] Most traveling is done by air, though the Council on Finance and Administration is increasing the auto mileage to 20 cents. Journeys that required days by train 30 years ago now can be made in a few hours. This should leave more time for study and leisure, but I fear it largely results in the acceptance of more engagements.

"Seventh, bishops today, as a whole, follow a more flexible plan of operation in making appointments than when I first started. Some of the bishops then had the reputation of being somewhat arbitrary in appointment making. It was said of Bishop Darlington that he 'carried his office in his hat,' and also that he was the last bishop to limit the use of his cabinet. I remember hearing him say, while consulting with the cabinet sometime near the close of an appointment making session, 'I have a list of five or six appointments.' He would pull the paper from his pocket, as he added quietly, 'These are episcopal appointments—we will not discuss them.'

"We did not have to place clergy couples, for there were none in those days, but we did have to face the problem of churches which paid only one salary but expected to be sent two church workers, both well qualified, the pastor and his wife.

"Eighth, in an earlier day, as the bishop presided in an Annual Conference he found many items being considered in the Conference as a whole. Now most matters go before standing committees, and are thrashed out there. The meetings of the committee on ministerial qualifications is less hush-hush than it used to be. I would say that the Annual Conference attempts much more for both preachers and people than used to be the case.

"Ninth, there is a decreased length of active service for most members of the Council of Bishops. This is because, I think, there is some tendency in the Jurisdictional Conferences to choose candidates who have fewer years to serve. Of course, the retirement age has been lowered twice in the last few years. In my judgment, a total active episcopacy of only eight years does not give a bishop a chance to contribute too much to the Church at the general level.

"There is a strong emphasis today upon the Council as a family, with very happy results. A large number of bishops exchange Christmas cards, and there is special recognition of anniversaries. The Council has a courtesy committee that sends flowers in case of serious illness or death of family members, and the bishops all contribute yearly. Each year there is a memorial service for bishops and wives and widows who have gone on during the current year. These services are always particularly tender family affairs."

BRIDGE BETWEEN THE PAST AND THE FUTURE

"I could go on and on writing about the changes in the Council of Bishops, leaving for another time some

THE BISHOPS' CHANGING ROLE IN A CHANGING CHURCH

word about changes in the Church. If, in any sense, I have been a link between the No More of the Past and the Not Yet of the Future, I am grateful for the privilege." (See chapter 22 on "Methodism, United, Has a Message.")

NOTES—SHORT AND LONG

1. See the latest General Minutes of the Annual Conferences, published under the general supervision of the Council of Finance and Administration for up-to-date figures on the number of churches with more than 3000 members. In 1978 there were 62, of which 51 were in the Southern Jurisdictions.
2. See the widely popular Abingdon Press paperback *United Methodism in Theory and Practice*, by Roy H. Short, published in 1974.
3. A few years ago there was a trend towards wearing clerical attire in formal meetings, though Bishop Short and a number of others never adopted it except overseas. At the same time the bishops went in for informal clothing at other times. On one occasion a bishop who ordinarily had on a clerical collar appeared in a flamboyant sports jacket. His bishop colleague across the aisle asked: "Do you have all your clothes cut out of horse blankets?"
4. At the Fall meeting, 1979, Bishop James Armstrong was absent because he was in Australia as consultant to the new united Church involving the Methodists there. Bishop Fred Wertz was in Czechoslovakia.

19

THE BISHOPS AND THE COUNCILS

The Council of Bishops and the Judicial Council are the only two of the four general councils mentioned in the Constitution of our Church. The other two are the Council of Finance and Administration, a most significant body that has changed its name to keep in step with the times; and the Council on Ministries, an Evangelical United Brethren gift to Methodism that has been greatly appreciated.[1]

Roy Short has had an important relationship to all four, and definite ideas about their place in our connectional system. He has always taken very seriously his part in making nominations.

Some of the members elected to the Judicial Council are nominated by the Council of Bishops, while others are elected from nominations made on the floor of the General Conference. Other than making such nominations, the bishops, through most of the last 40 years, have had little contact with the Judicial Council. And between the two Councils a certain gulf has existed, growing out of the responsibility of the Judicial Council to pass on decisions of the bishops. In most cases decisions of the bishops have been affirmed.

A local pastor and "church bureaucrat," as Dr. Hoover Rupert styles himself, has indicated some of the reasons why the two Councils have an affinity for each other. Let him tell how he first felt about the Judicial Council:

"When my bishop nominated me in 1968, I had mixed feelings. I thought of the Judicial Council as nine old men who dealt only with the dull, legislative technicalities of church law. When I was elected I set myself to endure this dullness for the coming years."[2]

Before long he was to discover that there were women members as well as men, and all were not necessarily old. There were professors and lawyers, and preachers, too. There were brilliant black leaders on the court.

"I was agreeably surprised to discover how much of the lifeblood of the Church flowed through the considerations which came to us. Indeed, it has been a fascinating experience, seldom dull, except in the reading of the third and fourth redrafts of a proposed decision." Then he goes on to say:

"What I was not really prepared for was the concern of bishops about the Judicial Council. We seemed to be a real threat to a few of your former members, now deceased. I can understand the reluctance to have a decisional matter before the Council when it might result in not being affirmed. Relatively few were overruled. Yet the *Discipline* has given us a function in governing the Church with its three branches of government—the executive in your Council, the legislative in the General Conference and the judicial in our Council."

A LIGHTNING ROD FOR THE BISHOPS

The Judicial Council secretary goes on to show that, as a service agency for the Church, his Council serves the bishops as a means of insuring that what we, as a Church, do in policy, program and organization is according to the Constitution. He continues:

THE BISHOPS AND THE COUNCILS

"In a sense we often 'take the rap' for you, making a final decision that relieves you, as a bishop, of that responsibility. There must be some sense of comfort for you in reminding a protesting Annual Conference leadership, 'I can't help it; the Judicial Council has ruled that it is unconstitutional to serve cocktails during Annual Conference coffee breaks!' "

He cites decisions on the issue of clergy couples as an instance of how the Judicial Council affirms the episcopal authority in matters of constitutionality and law. "Far from a threat to your judicial judgment, we see our function as one of support for you. And if you read thoroughly and thoughtfully the directions for bringing a matter before the Judicial Council, you will see that a primary route is through the Council of Bishops. In Paragraphs 2507 through 2514 of the *Discipline* the Council of Bishops is mentioned as a proper body to bring cases to the Judicial Council. No other church body is included in each paragraph.

"Besides, an individual bishop has the right of appeal to the Judicial Council in case of an adverse decision by a trial court. All other elders can make such appeal only on questions of law."

DEALING WITH EPISCOPAL FRUSTRATIONS

To continue with Secretary Rupert for a moment: "If I were a bishop I would find myself frustrated at times with the Judicial Council's apparent cavalier treatment of my Annual Conference's serious request for help from the Council. To be refused on a technicality and simply told, 'We cannot accept jurisdiction,' must be bothersome, even frustrating. Yet the *Discipline* clearly states the basis on which appeals can be made to the Judicial Council.

"We have had to turn back requests for help from Conference boards because their avenue of appeal lies through due process in the Annual Conference or through their parent general board. A recent rejection of jurisdiction denied an Annual Conference judicial assurance that their plan for electing delegates to General and Jurisdictional Conferences would not later come up for review."

TWO STANCES COURTS TAKE

"Let me share our problem with you. Traditionally, there are two different stances which courts of law maintain. One court will hear only those cases for which they can find no technical basis for nonjurisdiction. The court of another tradition will hear all cases for which they can find any possible legal basis for jurisdiction. You can assume that the former court will have many more nonjurisdictional declarations than the other.

"Both traditions would respond to the issue by pointing out that the *Discipline* offers clear delineation of the route by which cases come to the Judicial Council and when these are followed, jurisdiction is a mere formality.

"The Judicial Council has long been a low-profile organization. This, the current administration feels, is in part responsible for the lack of understanding of its place and function in the Church, and of the avenues of appeal which are properly open to its members and agencies. Thus, we are seeking to raise the profile while keeping the dignity of a high court."

"A CERTAIN PROPER DISTANCE"

Roy remembers one case in which, at the request of the Council of Bishops, two bishops appeared before the Judicial Council to request a review of a certain decision, and one or two of the members made it evident that they felt this to be out of order, and they excused themselves.

THE BISHOPS AND THE COUNCILS

In two instances the members of the Council of Bishops asked the Judicial Council to reconsider decisions. Roy reports:

"One was the decision holding that a term bishop, reaching retirement in office, was no longer a member of the Council of Bishops. The other decision held that a bishop cannot transfer a minister from one Conference to another without his consent. In both instances the request was denied.

"In recent years a new move to ease relationships has developed between the two Councils. At the invitation of the Council of Bishops Dr. Ralph Houston appeared before them. Since then it has not been unusual for the president and other members to visit the Council of Bishops. The current president, Tom H. Matheny, a distinguished Louisiana lawyer, has made it a habit to write the bishops as conditions may seem to warrant."[3]

THIS MATTER OF FINANCES

The bishops have always had important ties with the Council on Finance and Administration, and with its predecessor bodies in both the Methodist Church and the Evangelical United Brethren Church. It is this Council that recommends to the General Conference what the bishops' salaries are to be, and their housing and office allowances. (Incidentally, the Council has performed for the bishops certain services that it is not mandated to give, such as providing for the episcopal seals of office, and also seating for the bishops at General Conference and hospitality facilities.)

The Council on Finance and Administration administers the Episcopal Fund, raised from the Annual Conferences as a small fraction of ministerial salaries. The Council establishes travel allowances, both regular and special, payments for moving expenses, telephone, postage and office equipment and other expenses incident to the bishop's office. Of course, this Council pays the salaries of the bishops on the first of each month.

The membership of the Council is nominated and elected according to provisions in the *Discipline*. Since 1939 the president has always been a bishop[4] and there has been the custom of alternating the presidency among different sections of the Church, although this is not required. The Council has an episcopal committee on which no bishop is permitted to sit.

There has always been a cordial relationship between the secretary of the Council (who is also called the treasurer of the Church) and the Council of Bishops.[5]

A NEW COUNCIL—ON MINISTRIES

For 29 years after Methodist union in 1939, each board of The Methodist Church operated independently, subject only to the General Conference. Plans were developed by each board without consulting those of other boards, with the result that there was much overlapping and confusion. As might be expected, many local churches rebelled.

There was a provision in the *Discipline* for a Council of Secretaries, but they had no actual coordinating power. Meetings were largely times for conversation and fellowship, in which a clever secretary seldom disclosed what he and his associates were thinking and planning. Roy makes this comment out of his experience:

"The lack of coordination became so serious throughout the Church that something had to be done. For a long time, when a problem appeared, the pattern was to appoint a committee to try to work out differences between boards, but these inter-board committees were long on good intentions and short on achievements.

THE BISHOPS AND THE COUNCILS

"The Evangelical United Brethren Church had developed a Program Council to deal with the programmatic situation, and it was working well. The idea appealed to the Methodists and we were glad to have it adopted, in 1968, for the united Church.

"As the united Church moved into the new quadrennium it soon became apparent that operating a program council in a church the size of the former Evangelical United Brethren Church and a church as large as United Methodism were two different matters. The 1972 General Conference, therefore, eliminated the Program Council and brought into being the Council of Ministries."

Roy was a member of the Structure Committee that was charged with the responsibility of making proposals to the General Conference for reordering the total board structure of the Church. The committee entered into its work in good conscience, but in the third year of the quadrennium it had reached what seemed to be an impasse. Part of the situation centered around the proposed Council of Ministries. At the 1971 meeting Roy brought in a paper which the committee accepted, and it broke the deadlock.

The proposal, as he made it, was recommended to the General Conference, but changes were made in the committees which altered the original proposal considerably. It could be said, however, that the proposal did help to get the committee off dead center.

When the General Conference finally approved a Council of Ministries, Roy welcomed particularly the provisions for every Annual Conference to be represented in this important body. This was one of the features of his original proposal in the Structure Committee. Of course, he was disappointed in the provision that excluded a bishop being an officer of the Council. He felt this provision unjustified, since no other agency had such an exclusive provision, and the 1976 General Conference made an appropriate correction.

The relationships among the four Councils has been discussed at length in the church press. In the next chapter see some other issues that have been talked about.

NOTES—SHORT AND LONG

1. The Judicial Council is an outgrowth of a brilliant idea, founded on the checks and balances plan of American democracy. Our "judicial arm" was developed by the Methodist Episcopal Church, South.
2. This and succeeding quotations from Dr. Hoover Rupert come from a letter he wrote to members of the Council of Bishops in the fall of 1979.
3. One communication concerned the decision on a congregation's right to employ an avowed homosexual as pastor when the Annual Conference approved.
4. These bishops have chaired the Council: Ernest Lynn Waldorf, Titus Lowe, Clare Purcell, G. Bromley Oxnam, Paul Martin, and then, following the death of F. Gerald Ensley, Ellis Finger.
5. In The Methodist Church, beginning with 1939, the secretaries have been: Dr. O. W. Auman, Dr. Thomas B. Lugg, Dr. Don A. Cooke, and Dr. Bryan Brawner. Dr. Ewing Wayland has followed Dr. Brawner in the United Methodist Church.

20
USING, NOT ABUSING THE CHURCH PRESS

*M*ethodist history shows that there was another Editor Short besides Roy Short. He was Harry Short, who edited *The Kentucky Methodist* after Roy started the paper as a district news sheet. The news story was that the paper had "simply changed Shorts."

Roy did not have printer's ink in his veins, as the saying goes, but he had it under his fingernails—or would have, if he were not so fastidious about his appearance.[1] He has written half a dozen books—four of them since his retirement in 1972—and hundreds of articles for the church press, in which he profoundly believes. His reasoning is that it is, or should be, the press of the Church. It need not be owned by the Church officially, but it must be concerned about the causes that are close to the heart of the Church and its Lord. It should reveal both the mind of the Church, and help the Church make up its mind about pertinent matters.

STEWARDSHIP OF THE PRESS

Hear Roy's arguments as he spoke and wrote about the stewardship of writing and publishing skills in an address delivered at Nashville, on the title, "*Together* and Connectionalism."

USING, NOT ABUSING THE CHURCH PRESS

"I am afraid that all too few of us in our modern day realize the actual importance of the Church paper in the ongoing life of any church. Apparently, our fathers, with their great devotion to the periodicals of the Church knew this better than we do. Even those of us who are preachers often look at the church paper as an optional something which our people may take or not take as they choose—just as they do *Time* or *Reader's Digest* or any other of the hundreds of publications which are available on every hand."

Then he goes into the history of church papers:

"There are churches which have been born as a result of a religious paper. Such was the case with one of three churches merged in 1939 to form our own Methodist Church. One hundred years before that there had been widely circulated a religious paper known as *Mutual Rights*. Making its appearance amid the democratic fervor of the Jacksonian era, it took its stand for lay rights and for democracy in the Church. Out of its arousal of the people The Methodist Protestant Church came into being.

"There are churches whose onward and upward and outward thrust has been spearheaded consistently by some church paper which, by its very nature, has proved itself the banner moving out ahead of the marching hosts of the general church membership. For a century and more the *Advocates* of Methodism were exactly what their name indicates—the champions of great causes to which they sought to rally the devotion and energies of the Church. A fascinating approach to the wide sweep of Methodist history for a hundred years could be had by way of a paper centering around Methodism's great editors and their significant contributions."[2]

Roy continues with his third point about the Church's dependence on the church paper:

"There are even churches which appear to find their center of gravity in a church paper. There is one large and growing denomination whose activities largely come to focus in this city.³ which seems to find its cohesiveness largely in a church paper. It has no general boards, no general office or staff, and it acknowledges no centralization of activities in anything approaching a general conference or a national convention, yet it moves with an unusual degree of unity which is not altogether, of course, but to no inconsiderable degree, due to the leadership given to a respected and well circulated periodical."

WHEN PASTORS PROMOTE THE PAPER

Even in the days of radio and television, breathtaking wonders of communication, Roy is sure about the need for church papers going into the homes of as many people as possible.

"Methodism has always been a connectional church," he wrote in the days when *Together* was a "bold, new venture." "This has been our strength in the yesterday, and many of us believe this can still be our strength in the tomorrows. But never were there greater strains upon our connectionalism than right now. Our very bigness puts a strain on our connectionalism. . . . Our dispersion over all sections of the United States and in 40 countries around the world with our membership including rich and poor, university graduates and people who have not finished the grades, puts a strain on our connectionalism. . . . The pressing issues of the times in which we live puts another strain on our connectionalism, because these must be faced and the Church cannot close its eyes to them." He continues:

"Reaction to social issues is usually diverse, and our people are caught up in the pros and cons of every major issue. Sometimes this makes for suspicion and distrust, and congregations as well as larger groups of Methodists find themselves sharply divided.⁴

USING, NOT ABUSING THE CHURCH PRESS

"In the midst of these strains upon connectionalism we are trying, at many points, to be connectional without a connecting means. We do have our Conference system—with its unified administration and its interrelated ministry—but relatively few of our people are in touch with this system at its chief focal points such as the General Conference sessions, the Annual Conference sessions and our Quarterly Conference sessions.

"We do have great institutions such as our colleges and universities and our hospitals and homes which, in a sense, become limited rallying centers in the life of our Church, but all too many of our members are scarcely aware of the existence of our institutions.

"We do have our church-school literature prepared by a single Curriculum Committee and, theoretically, essentially one in its philosophy, but it is necessarily graded and, therefore, used only by particular groups at particular times.[5] Its final effect when it is used over a period of considerable time may be a certain desired impact, but it offers no quick and direct way to get all our constituency at once.

"We do have our respective boards, agencies and organizations, all of them doing effective work, but each of them inevitably tends to reach only part of the people with a particular emphasis.

"If the connectionalism of Methodism is to be preserved in any vital way, somehow the Church must continue to reach down into the homes of Methodism and reach Methodists individually with something of a unified appeal."

Two bishops, named by the Council of Bishops, have always met with the Board of Publication, which makes substantive decisions for the United Methodist Publishing House. Too often, however, these bishops have not been advised of editorial and promotional policies, even though bishops have long been regarded as key figures in the circulation problems of church papers. All of the bishops have received representatives of our publishing interests and given them the privilege of the floor at Annual Conferences. One happy purpose of these visits has been to present checks in accordance with Article VI of the Constitution.[6]

In the paper mentioned, Bishop Short, spokesman for warm-hearted Methodism, ticked off some suggestions for making the general church paper a supporter of connectionalism. He wrote:

"We are in the midst of a quadrennium in which, as Methodists, we are committed to the idea of becoming more truly one Church, both within our own ranks, and with all others who love the Lord Jesus Christ in sincerity and truth, than we have been heretofore. It is difficult to imagine any one single thing that can more effectively challenge our people to one witness in one world than a family paper, strongly committed to the Church's mission in this hour of the world's life, going into the homes of our people everywhere."

COMMUNICATIONS: WHOLESALE AND RETAIL

The discussion of the plan to abandon a general church publication in favor of a general source of information and inspiration for both print and electronics (radio and television) media was heated, and the General Conference of 1976 produced a Commission on Communications, with Annual, District and Local Church connections. It assumed that an overall communications system was called for—some persons and groups even called very loudly.

The terms "wholesale" and "retail" bring to mind an old Rotarian joke about the pastor who belonged to the club and the new district superintendent who had moved to town and was willing to join. Both had to have different classifications. "I know," said the president, fumbling with his gavel. "One of you can be classified as 'Religion: Wholesale' and the other as 'Religion: Retail.' "

The fiction that United Methodism can be divided into "local" and "general" is heresy in our connectionalism. The *Discipline* to the contrary notwithstanding, there is no such thing as a "local" church nor, for that matter, a "general" church. A Methodist congregation that forgets its worldwide connections, opportunities and obligations or gives over its total world parish contributions into other hands is no true Methodist church.

According to Roy, another direction indicator warns us of the fallacy of trying to divide religion into wholesale and retail. (God forbid that faith could ever be bought and sold in the commodities market!) That would be almost as bad as trying to segregate the "religious press" from the "working press" at the United Nations, or to label some printing machines "religious" and some "secular" (for tax purposes, of course) in a church printing plant.[7]

Some questions occurred to Roy and others: Admitted that the United Methodist Church, with its skilled news-gatherers and news-organizers and news-interpreters could provide features, news articles, syndicated columns, pictures and such, who would supervise the selection for its possible interest to church members? Who would check the "sources"? If the news is to be published by Methodist editors, newscasters and radio commentators while it is still news, how is it to be processed and sent out? In wholesale and retail terminology, what will be the "markup" between the cost of wholesale news and retail news? For example, will some news be sent to *The New World Outlook* and some other news to the Evangelicals' *Good News?*

The development of a communications "system" is vastly important, if it can be founded on a genuine appreciation of philosophy—some would say a theology—of communications. This is the heart of the matter. It is much more important than the problem of dealing with sibling rivalries between the institutional children of the Church, or the sons and daughters in various parts of the world, who have already become their own publishers, or even the conflicts between communications with type and those with tubes.

Roy thinks this is a fascinating task for the young fellows!

USING, NOT ABUSING THE
CHURCH PRESS

NOTES—SHORT AND LONG

1. Bishop Earl G. Hunt, Jr., says: "His demeanor upon all public ecclesiastical occasions has always been the soul of propriety and even somber sobriety. But to see him emceeing a game and contest period at a cabinet meeting or a staff retreat, some sort of foolish headgear established jauntily above his white locks, would cause any Methodist preacher to do a startled double-take!"
2. When T. Otto Nall was editor of the Northwestern-Central editions of *The Christian Advocate* he studied the files to discover the issues that were highlighted at 10-year intervals. The study showed that church papers were aware of and spoke out on current issues.
3. The city is Nashville, and the denomination the Church of Christ.
4. *Together* made a valiant, if belated effort to present the burning issues of the sixties in the days when the Church was plagued with division that resulted in parties, cliques and caucuses. New papers, like *The United Methodist Reporter* came along to try to "ventilate the Methodist mind."
5. The revolution in church-school materials and methods was reflected in the Curriculum Committee, chaired by Bishops Harmon and Nall. A cooperative, interdenominational project that included 16 denominations published a thick book *The Church's Educational Ministry, a Curriculum Plan*. It recommends the latest methods.
6. Article VI of the Church's Constitution reads: "The General Conference shall not appropriate the net income of the publishing houses, the book concerns, or the Chartered Fund for any other purpose than for the benefit of retired or disabled preachers, their spouses, widows or widowers and children and other beneficiaries of the ministerial pension system."
7. This actually happened in the Methodist Publishing House plant at Cincinnati, Ohio, in the thirties.

21
FELLOWSHIPING WITH OTHER FAITHS

A stalwart dedication to the Wesleyan heritage with its simple tastes[1] and abstemious habits did not keep Roy from fellowship with others who did not follow such strict regimens. Bishop Earl G. Hunt, Jr., makes these comments:

"For the most part, his clothing has always been severely and even painfully clerical—although it should be noted, he has revealed latent tendencies to sartorial wildness in the acquisition of an off-white shirt, a brown suit and what at least faintly resembled a paisley tie.[2]

"He is a connoisseur of good foods, with what must surely be an exquisitely sensitive palate, but his culinary preferences sometimes plunge to plebeian depths, and include white bacon and grits. I recall one time when he spent a delightful period recounting the number of delicious dishes which could be contrived with a grits base. I remember another and memorable occasion when both of us were at the Bellevue Stratford Hotel in Philadelphia for a church meeting, and he squired me away at noon to a picturesque nearby haunt known as 'Oyster Alley' where we sat together in a crowded little restaurant enjoying the finest of oyster stew served family style!

"His native neatness has surely been one of the easier explanations for his remarkable administrative efficiency. His library is carefully pruned and contains only the books which he cherishes, particularly his unusual and valuable collection of biographies of the bishops. His desk is clean, and a letter received one day is usually responded to before the next. The unusual amount of traveling involved in his responsibility as secretary of the Council of Bishops has caused him to keep a bag already packed and prepared for a journey available at all times. His experience in tripping about over the world has taught him what he may never have been able successfully to communicate to his wife—the advantage of traveling light!"

MEETINGS, EVERYWHERE WITH EVERYBODY

A large fraction of Roy's traveling over the years has been done because of his ecumenical interests and responsibilities. What would be a burden and a bore to many has been a joy to him. As a young preacher he was active in his own city and in the state council of churches. A delegate to the World Council of Churches meeting in New Delhi, India, (1937) he was surprised when, at its conclusion, he was named to the Central Committee. He served for 10 years, attending all meetings except for the year when he transferred from Kentucky to Florida.

Roy's assignment on this directing body of the World Council was the sub-committee on finance. He was a vice-chairman when the famed Martin Niemöller was chairman and gave distinguished leadership. The list of meeting places included Paris, Rochester, Geneva, Crete and elsewhere. He was a member of the general assembly when the Council held its eventful meeting in Uppsala.

For almost all of his episcopal career Roy was also a member of the executive committee of the National Council of Churches of Christ in the U.S.A., and for six years he headed the nominating committee. In fact, he was chairman when

Bishop Reuben Mueller, then of the Evangelical United Brethren Church, was named president. (As noted, in chapter 13, "Ecumenicity—Beginning with Us," he treasured most the assignment with the World Methodist Council and attended all of its world sessions.)

PLUSES AND MINUSES OF COUNCIL MOVEMENTS

Roy was in a policy-making position long enough to observe the advantages and disadvantages of the Council pattern on both national and international scales. Promises and perils, you might say, for the future.

He rejoiced to see the temptation avoided to become a world church, with a rigid doctrine and discipline, and the status of a council maintained. He had his doubts about some of the political moves, even on issues that had general approval. He wondered whether meetings of representatives of churches from all nations should become a debating society, a United Nations association at prayer.

He viewed with alarm the trend towards paternalism on the part of the Western churches in dealing with younger churches. The father-knows-best attitude is as bad on an international level as in a local situation, he believes. He has opposed handing over hard-earned mission funds to interdenominational agencies without any accounting to member churches, and he has short patience with the policy of some denominations planting "seed money" and other denominations picking up the tab for fertilizing, cultivating and harvesting without an interest in anything but the "gleaning" in the corners.[3]

WHEN CHURCH UNION FALTERS

Among the bright and bold dreams of the times in which Roy has planned and worked is the church union movement that had its origin in early Christian history. One of its most dramatic expressions is found in what was bravely begun by Episcopal Bishop James A. Pike and Dr. Eugene Carson Blake, Presbyterian top executive who became secretary of the World Council of Churches. The Committee on Church Union (popularly known by its acronym "COCU") is one of its most promising results. In one paper for the bishops in 1967 Roy said:

"COCU appears to envision less of a church than we now know, in some respects. It would be a large church embodying various traditions, but it would essentially be a big American church. It would, of course, support endeavors in mission through the world, but the sending and receiving patterns would be here. Methodism, however, has been, until now, one world church in its conception and functioning, however imperfect this may have been. That vision is fading, but it is still there for many of us."

Unquestionably, Roy remembers the story about John Wesley's visit to Heaven, and his attempt to find the Methodists there.[4] His guide around the celestial precincts pointed out this group and that, each enjoying its own special kind of worshipping, serving, talking, fellowshipping and working. (Yes, even in Heaven!) But the founder of Methodism, who never left the Anglican communion in this life, even though he was forbidden to preach in their churches, kept insisting on finding out what rewards there were for those who had joined his bands and class meetings.

"Where are the Methodists?" he asked.

"Oh, Reverend Father, we have no Methodists here," the guide said. "We are all merely Christians."

For a variety of reasons, the Commission on Church Union has had a rough time gaining and losing members from the original nine. There has been much giving up of this for that, with the Episcopalians and Methodists holding fast to the episcopacy, even though they are not together on how bishops have come to be what they are. The real issue, of course, is the image of the Church in this changing world. Back in 1967 Roy wrote for the Council of Bishops a paper on "Characteristics of the Methodist Episcopacy." He said:

"Methodists have themselves always felt free to criticize the episcopacy, and at times they have put new curbs upon it; and yet they have held on to it, and they continue so to do. This is not because of any great reverence for the episcopacy as such, but because of its functional role in meeting the needs of the churches. . . .

"We do not quarrel to preserve an office, but we do have great concern for that which, in the Methodist system, the episcopacy guarantees, namely the care of all the churches, large and small, and all the ministry of the Church, gifted and less gifted. Before laying aside a system which has been found workable, and continues to be found workable, we would be anxious to know what provision is proposed for equally efficient care for both all the churches and all the ministry.

"As Methodists we could scarcely settle without grave misgivings for an episcopacy represented largely by a title, essentially an order, reduced largely to an arrangement for pastoral care, stripped of the power to function quickly and efficiently in the interest of the ministry; and held together so loosely as not to be able to function efficiently as a total administrative unit serving the total Church."

OUR EPISCOPACY AND ITINERANCY

After the 1976 General Conference ordered that a Study Commission on Itinerancy be set up to suggest Disciplinary provisions for clergy couples, part-time appointments, the worker-priest concept of ministry and how guaranteed employment for Conference members "affects these and other matters of clergy morale," the commission began by going back to the fundamentals of the itinerant system. Their study of Methodist history led them to these conclusions:

"Methodism began as a missionary movement, and its strategies and structures developed as a means of fulfilling that missionary vocation. The United Methodist Church continues in its heritage of connectional policy, the essence of which is that every church is a part of every other church, and that no one church can live to itself alone. . . .

"The simple essence of an itinerant ministry is a disciplined and directed mobility of preachers in the interests of fulfilling the evangelical mission of the Church. The system promises that each church will be provided ministerial leadership, and that each minister will be provided a field of labor. . . . It requires that each charge receive and support the minister appointed, and that each minister must go to and serve faithfully the appointed field of labor. Itinerancy involves a convenanted commitment on the part of congregations, clergy and connection. . . .

"United Methodism makes no claim of scriptural mandate for the system of itineracy, but does cite scriptural example growing out of the 'great commission' to discipleship. Itineracy was conceived and has developed as a pragmatic response to the Church's missional vocation. . . .

"The itinerant system involves a missional ministry which is a sacrificial ministry. It requires full commitment of the minister, including whatever sacrifices may be required, to be a servant under orders with priority pledged to the mission of the church. Itinerant ministry in The United Methodist Church is not a natural religious right of anyone—it is a covenantal ministry. . . ."

Within these guidelines, which followers of Wesley would be unwilling to abandon, the commission has worked out some new paragraphs to be considered for the 1980

Discipline. They add:

"The Commission asks the Division of Ordained Ministry to see that one session of the training for new district superintendents and new bishops be spent on sensitizing to vital issues in itineracy and training of Pastor-Parish Relations committees."

FELLOWSHIPING WITH OTHER FAITHS

NOTES—SHORT AND LONG

1. Bishop Short still doubts that he, a retired bishop, ought to be driving a Cadillac, even though it came to him by way of a relative.
2. This fastidious habit of dressing makes him a genuine follower of Father Wesley who emerged from scuffles with mobs with every lock of his white wig in place and his pulpit robe, though well worn, spotlessly clean.
3. The reference, which might be footnoted with "chapter and verse" many times over, refers to the practice among some denominations to start a school or clinic or camp with "seed money" and, after planting it, depart, leaving the fertilizing and cultivating to others.
4. This story has been variously credited. According to Dr. Oscar Thomas Olson, of the World Methodist Council, it was told by a black leader in a World Council of Churches meeting. The humor of it is obvious, for the writer of Wesley's "Letter to a Catholic" would never have been so parochial.

22
METHODISM, UNITED, HAS A MESSAGE

*B*ishop Paul Kern, who spoke at Epworth League Day in the Century of Progress program, Chicago in 1934, wrote a book entitled *Methodism Has a Message*. There have been many books, large and small, that attempted to say that "Methodism has a method." That was the hope of John and Charles Wesley, who formed the Holy Club at Oxford, and the method, as well as the dedicated motivation and the unperishable message have kept Methodism alive.

Roy Short, as an episcopal leader over 24 years, and even today in retirement, has had a part in thinking out and writing those messages. He thinks they may be summarized, not in such a statement as "God lives and all's right with the world," but rather something like "God loves and we work to make his will known and followed everywhere."

Bishop James K. Mathews, present secretary of the Council of Bishops, recently put in the hands of the Council of Bishops 22 messages beginning with a statement on the world situation in 1939, the year of Methodist Unification, and concluding with the mid-quadrennial message, 1978. The occasion for the publication was the 40th anniversary of the Council of Bishops.

Roy Short says: "The messages of the Council represent

METHODISM, UNITED, HAS A MESSAGE

our common opinion and, with some exceptions by Central Conference bishops, were signed by all."

Bishop Mathews explains that the messages are wide-ranging. They deal with theological topics, social ethics and many pragmatic matters of concern to the churches. They are really pastoral letters addressed mainly to the laity and clergy of our denomination, but always of such nature as to be overheard by the world. They are not the longish "state of the church" messages addressed to the General Conferences.

A few paragraphs offer some hints of trends and tendencies over the years since the Uniting Conference:

ON THE WORLD SITUATION—DECEMBER 9, 1939

> To a confused world, the Church proclaims the certainties of the centuries:
>
> To men of might who rule for a little hour, the Church declares, "Jesus Christ shall become the Ruler of the Kings of the Earth."
>
> To men drunk with power, who vainly place their trust in force, the Church repeats, "Blessed are the meek: for they shall inherit the earth" (Matt. 5:5).
>
> To self-appointed "leaders" who ignore the will of their own people and coerce the consciences of other peoples, the Church asserts, "One is your Leader, even the Christ."
>
> To mad dictators, who cry "Woe to the weak," the Church replies, "He who would be greatest among you must become the Servant of All" (Mark 9:35, paraphrase).

WAR-TIME MESSAGE TO THE CHURCH, DECEMBER 12, 1941

> For the sincere conscientious objector we have invoked and defended that right (of freedom of conscience). We will continue to do so.

By this, however, it was not intended, nor is it now intended, to commit the Church to efforts to persuade our youth to take this position inasmuch as the Church, as a Church, should not be used for military recruiting. . . .

There is no inconsistency in wholehearted devotion as Christian citizens to the immediate task, and the desire and determination to keep the Church, as a Church, free from participation or entanglement in the clashing activities of war. . . .

THE UN-CHRISTLIKE CHARACTER OF WAR,
DECEMBER 7, 1942

We are under no illusion regarding the un-Christlike character of war as a method of settling international disputes. Nor do we forget our own shortcomings and sins relative to the conditions that produced this struggle. But we are in the midst of it now because there has arisen in the world a philosophy driven by unchristian motives and bent upon establishing its will upon mankind. Against the idealogy and its supporters the United Nations have set themselves with grim determination. We pledge ourselves to the destruction of this brutal and unwarranted aggression and to the preservation for all mankind of the sacred liberties of free peoples. . . .

LOOKING BACK ON METHODIST UNION,
JANUARY 17, 1952

Thirteen years have passed since the consummation of Methodist union. What we did well apart, we now do better together. Methodism has the message, the numerical strength and the opportunity to launch a bold spiritual offensive, and it is our hope and prayer that we may be fully prepared to interpret Christ to the inquiring mind and seeking heart of this generation. . . .

The Church must take into account the world atmosphere in which it lives and works. For a decade, widespread and multiple tensions have produced serious frustrations within races, nations and individuals. All this especially affects our youth. The Church is challenged to speak to this condiction. . . .

ON GUILT BY ASSOCIATION, DECEMBER 11, 1953

In this time of fear and irresponsibile accusation, areas of freedom of speech and thought are being narrowed all over the world. In communist lands, thought control uses the techniques of absolute censorship, spying of secret police, torture, imprisonment and death.

In our land, where we protest against such types of control, self-appointed guardians of the liberty we want for ourselves and for all men may, by the calling of names, unfounded accusations, and the assertion of guilt by association, destroy the priceless heritage they claim to defend. In the United States today, there are people—some of them in our Church—who are being made to believe false statements about their leaders until the human mind is filled with suspicion and the human spirit is shackled.

In such an atmosphere suspicion becomes fear, fear becomes hatred, and hatred sets man against his neighbor, friend and brother. . . .

UNITED NATIONS AS A WAY TO PEACE,
APRIL 29, 1954

The assembling of the World Council of Churches is, over and above its manifold ministries, a symbol of great significance.... The United Nations is also a symbol. It serves to remind us that there is another kinship besides the brotherhood of faith—it is the brotherhood of a universal need and yearning, and it embraces all mankind. The people of every land and race are attempting to find a way to economic security and justice and freedom and peace.

The soul of this modern parliament of man is a sense of humanity's essential oneness in its basic needs and yearnings. We confidently believe that divisions that sometimes appear so threatening to a man's well-being can best be settled around a common council table, and that the United Nations is our best hope for world peace....

OF EVANGELISM IN OUR HERITAGE,
NOVEMBER 20, 1954

This (evangelism) has been and is now the supreme goal of all our endeavors. Since Methodist union in 1939, the Church has grown by nearly two million members. In all our history there has never been a time that our evangelistic programs have been more widespread than just now. Yet we take no undue satisfaction in our statistical victories, but we seek the commitment and devotion which will give us more spiritual power.

Let us pray humbly that the spiritual children of John Wesley—the ministers and laymen of The Methodist Church—may make their rightful contribution to a dark time which longs for the light of Jesus Christ.

NO FREEDOM UNTIL ALL ARE FREE,
DECEMBER 12, 1956

The tragic events in Hungary have brought into bold relief practices that are inherent in the philosophy upon which totalitarian tyranny is based. The heroic Hungarians who struck down the hand of the oppressor for a brief hour, were once again subjugated by ruthless and overwhelming force, but they stand in their suffering as symbols of the spirit that lives forever in the hearts of men created to breathe free. . . .

Revolution at present may be the only way for Hungarians and others, as it was for the United States in its early history. Reform that leans toward justice may be possible where freedom lives. But revolution and reform without regeneration will not do. It is a new spirit that must infuse mankind. The world must be reborn.

METHODISM NEEDS A NEO-WESLEYANISM,
APRIL 10, 1958

John Wesley was not a man to underestimate the sinfulness of man, but he knew man could be redeemed. Now, however, a strange theology has been infiltrating our thought. It results in passive and patient acceptance of injustice and of exploitation and calls upon man to await God's good time, and thus become a tool of reaction and a suffocating miasma. Its proponents seem to forget that man is to be a coworker with God and, together, to bring peace to warring humanity.

Neo-orthodoxy is neither new nor orthodox. Methodism needs a Neo-Wesleyanism. . . .

JUVENILE DELIQUENCY AND ALCOHOLISM,
NOVEMBER 13, 1958

Because alcoholic beverages have contributed materially to the alarming increase in juvenile delinquency we urge all workers with youth to refrain from the use of intoxicants because it is difficult to train young people in abstinence when their teachers, elders and employers drink. In the light of recent endorsements of the moderate use of alcoholic beverages, we reaffirm the Methodist position, which is total abstinence. We urge abstainers to stand firm, sure that such a witness will at least convince others that the practice of drinking is not unanimous. . . .

ON PRIVATE AND PAROCHIAL SCHOOLS,
APRIL 6, 1961

The proposal to use public tax funds for the support of primary and secondary sectarian parochial schools, either in the form of subsidy or loans, has now been lifted and its supporters have vowed that they will bring their influence to bear upon members of Congress to include this provision in the legislation granting federal financial assistance to education. . . . We deplore such action. . . .

We call upon our ministers, lay leaders and agencies to acquaint our Methodist constituency with the Methodist position on this issue and the reasons which support it; to inform legislators before whom such proposals shall come of their intention to work to maintain the separation of church and state in the field of education as it has been interpreted from the founding of our Republic. . . .

ABOUT NUCLEAR WARFARE AND PANIC PROGRAMS,
NOVEMBER 16, 1961

We warn against the folly of panic programs for bomb shelters. This, we believe, invites surrender to the assumption that nuclear conflict is inevitable; encourages irresponsible, even reckless action by national leaders; makes for indifference to the suffering a nuclear war and its aftermath would inflict upon defenseless and innocent people unable to avail themselves of protection; and develop a climate of hysteria which makes for war.

We call for a careful study by qualified national authorities before any all-out building program is promoted. We believe the best shelter program is that which is directed toward eradicating the causes of strife.

CHURCH POSITION ON RACIAL TENSION,
APRIL 18, 1963

We are a world church and proudly claim all peoples among our membership, all races under our banner.

At this time, we wish particularly to commend our Methodist ministers and laymen of the racially troubled areas of the world for the sincere and honest efforts that many have made and are making to improve relations between the races. We strongly urge that such efforts be continued, with particular emphasis being given to the right of all people, of all races, to enjoy full citizenship in this nation and every nation in God. . . .

No one has a monopoly on the best methods to attain the goals aimed at. Our main concern is that we be Christian in this and all other relationships of life.

RACE AND CHURCH MEMBERSHIP,
NOVEMBER 13, 1963

We urge our pastors, upon whom rests the responsibility of receiving persons into the Church to receive all who are qualified and who desire to be received, without regard to race, color, or national origin, and we individually and collectively pledge them our support as they do so. The Methodist Church is an inclusive church.

We decry, on legal as well as Christian grounds, the denial to any person of any color or race the right of membership or the right to worship in any Methodist church. Further, to move to arrest any persons attempting to worship is to us an outrage.

We call upon all Methodist institutions where such has not been done to bring their racial policies and practices in line with the Christian principles of racial inclusiveness to which we are committed.

TO VATICAN COUNCIL II, APRIL 21, 1965

From our side we know full well that the ecumenical pathway on which you and we also have set our feet is long and arduous—and the end is not yet in sight. But on such a pathway, as in all other providential journeys, the pilgrim People of God walk by faith and not sight. . . .

We permit ourselves the liberty to intimate to you, most respectfully, our especial concern for some of the issues still on the Council's agenda for consideration and judgment. We assume that you understand the profound importance we attach to a clear and firm declaration on religious liberty, not only as a premise for the decree *On Ecumenism,* but as a demonstration of the Council's good faith in its program as a whole.

In addition, we eagerly await your actions on Roman Catholic-non-Roman Catholic Christian relations, the proposed constitution *On Divine Revelation* and the crucial schema of "The Presence of the Church in the Modern World." In these days of preparation for the fourth session of the Council and during its progress, we shall be joining our prayers with you for God's gracious blessing and guidance in all your deliberations.

METHODISM, UNITED, HAS A MESSAGE

ABOUT RECONCILIATION, NOVEMBER 18, 1965

Nothing seems more important in the world order than the ministry of reconciliation—the restoration to harmony and friendship. It is not enough to identify the ills, analyze the causes, enact legislation for correction and wait for results. Some ground rules are necessary, but an alert spontaneity to practice the Spirit of Christ speaks more effectively than many courts of law. Ultimate victory is in Christian love for which the Church is largely responsible with respect to effort and life. There is no substitute for its constant practice.

This emphasis on reconciliation is needed in worldwide areas of conflict as well as in the local situation. The recent progress made in the field of human relations and the new dignity given to all of God's children in many lands must go further than "obedience to law" and "recognition of human rights." Not only will the prayers of Christian people avail much, but every intelligent, peaceful gesture should be exhausted by the good people of the world that brothers and sisters may help each other, not exploit and kill. The voice of the Church has a place with civic, fraternal and governmental agencies in the program for peace.

WAR IN VIETNAM, NOVEMBER 16, 1967

We are concerned about the effect of the Vietnam war in worsening the international situation. The survival of civilization depends on the establishment of a climate of acceptance and cooperation among world powers. It is clear that the resolution of the Vietnam war is a major prerequisite if such a climate is to be established. We are confident that the best interests of all nations require that the escalation of the conflict be halted quickly.

At the moment, each side indicates the possibility of action if the other side acts first. The sterile rounds of demand and counter demand, accompanied by steady escalation by the parties to the conflict, must be broken by fresh and creative action by one of the parties. We believe that the United States should take this initiative.

ON THE CONFLICT OF GENERATIONS, APRIL 9, 1969

Young people are displaying their disdain for global injustices, the hypocrisy of affluent societies which articulate high values but do not live by them, impersonal bureaucracies, and the dehumanizing effects of technology. Most of them are sensitive and responsible; a small minority has followed a course of purposeless destruction.

These young people have their counterparts in the older generation. Most of their seniors sincerely try to understand new ideas and inevitable change; some, however, remain unreasonably threatened and inflexible.

The generation gap is no new phenomenon. History shows that generational conflict often has been more creative than destructive. . . .

OF DIVISIONS IN SOCIETY, NOVEMBER 13, 1969

Reconciliation is the basic fact of the gospel of Jesus Christ. Revolution is a reality of our time. Often the two seem irreconcilable. Today society is dangerously divided; black and white, rich and poor, left and right, old and young, city and countryside, pietist and secularist. Many of us are ill-prepared to cope with the angry voices and strident demands of the hour. We do not understand them. We are threatened by them. . . .

The violent Marxism of the Black Manifesto is utterly

METHODISM, UNITED, HAS A MESSAGE

unacceptable to United Methodists. No less intolerable for us is the continued injustice and deprivation which multitudes of men suffer both in our nation and in other parts of the world. . . .

"Black power" when responsibly used, does not call for violence, but rather full participation in political, social, religious and economic life that the black man might develop self-respect and pride in race. The same principle applies to "red" and "brown power" movements as American Indians and Spanish-speaking Americans seek justice and equality.

The Christian will, therefore, try to understand and interpret the phenomenon of "black separatism," not as an expression of Christian idealism, but as a pathway chosen by some black Americans to reach their personal and racial goals. While not presuming to judge a strategy that has grown out of humiliation and pain, we must earnestly and prayerfully work for the day when all will be done in Christ and strive for a society genuinely recognizing justice for all. . . .

FOR PENITENT THANKSGIVING, NOVEMBER 15, 1973

America is hurting and the pain runs deep. What enemies without could not achieve we have brought upon ourselves. The heart of the Republic pounds angrily one moment, subsides to a murmur of indifference the next. Whence the sickness? In part we have been damaged by our strength. Hard work and personal ambition made the nation rich and strong. But now personal ambition and acute self-interest in high places have lost government its credibility and blurred for us the founders' vision.

Whence the sickness? We suffer in part from a lack of the sense of the Holy. God has been reduced to three letters stamped upon a coin. The piety we warm to focuses on the world within and the world to come; it rarely notices the present world out there. A God thus disengaged from history becomes captive to the national interest. Righteousness becomes a matter of expediency. Justice lies fallen in the street.

We believe that our sickness need not be fatal. Democracy is still our best hope. . . .

But the nation's sickness is moral and spiritual as well as political, and the churches share responsibility for it. President Jefferson said, "I tremble for my country when I reflect that God is just." Our collective misdeeds will inescapably bring upon us a collective retribution, but God is merciful as well as just and will forgive those who sincerely repent and change their lives so that they no longer merit retribution.

THE STATE OF THE CHURCH IN OUR WORLD,
MARCH 31, 1978

It is possible to view the church—the whole Church of our own denomination—with eyes of despair. In some lands it is indeed sorely persecuted and its survival is threatened. In other societies an effort is made to stifle and suffocate the Church by ignoring it. In some instances secularism has taken over. In some places and in some ways, we confess, the Church has failed to be an agent of transformation and renewal. It has refused to be the body of Christ.

It has not sought renewal of resources for personal spiritual commitment and empowerment. It has turned back to ancient heresies, in the guise of new movements, for false comfort and confidence. It has sought to save its own life in an illusory quest for safety and security; it has withdrawn within its own walls. Too often its witness has been blunted by a comfortable accommodation to its own cultural setting while its preoccupation with internal concerns has thwarted its engagement with the needs of humanity. However penitent God's people ought to be and however grievous all our failures must be to our Lord, the Church is nevertheless his Body; the world is God's world.

This same world shows signs of awakening. On a global scale there is nowadays an explosion of awareness and a seeking after fullness of humanity. It may be observed everywhere; among the youth, the students, among women, the poor, ethnic minorities. Throughout the Third World there is a reaching out for life. There is a universal search and longing for justice and equality, for meaning and community, for stability, for truth, for life itself. If people want a fuller life, that is precisely the gift Jesus came to offer. . . .

So it is that the Church is discovering that its contemporary setting is in reality one that is abundant in its promise as well as a great challenge and responsibility to the People of God.

23

HONORING THE METHODIST HERITAGE

*R*oy tells the story of an unforgettable visit he made to a little church that hugged the side of one of the Blue Ridge Mountains of Virginia:

"I had been invited to preach at Fort Blackmore. After I preached they had dinner on the grounds. An old mountain layman came up to me and said, 'You know you're not the first bishop that's been here. . . .' 'Who was the other bishop?' 'Well, we've heard the old folks talk about him. His name was Asbury.' Of course the old man did not realize that this had been 150 years ago. The church had been passing the word on for all this time." Bishop Short checked Asbury's personal journal, and he had been in the Virginia mountains at Blackmore at the time.

"Episcopal biography has been one of my enthusiasms," Roy says. "I have read every biography of a Methodist bishop I could get my hands on. There are a dozen of them that have been written by other bishops, though ours here is only the second by a bishop biographer when the subject of the biography was still living."[1] Roy continues:

"The history of our American Methodism is written in the thinking and living of its episcopal leaders, and I know the same may be said for the history of the former Evangelicals and United Brethren. And, for the last quadrennium of my

HONORING THE METHODIST HERITAGE

active episcopacy I had the privilege of serving as president of the Commission of Archives and History."

HISTORIANS AND THE HERITAGE

Roy is not so much an antiquarian, who fancies old books, simply because they are first editions, or old copies of periodicals that have long since ceased publication, or the badges that bishops wore at General Conferences.[2] Nor is he essentially the fancier or collector of antiques representing certain periods in the lives of church leaders and organizations.[3] He is exceedingly interested in discovering the location of landmarks and preserving shrines.

He is not an archivist who performs the important function of restoring the decaying documents, both private and public, that are of historical importance. "I hope that we shall soon have a place where valuable records of our past can be studied by scholars who are attempting to write our history," he says. "And I look forward to much writing being done during the 1980-84 quadrennium, reaching ahead to the 200th anniversary of the Christmas Conference that started American Methodism at Lovely Lane Chapel in Baltimore back in 1784."

He is an historian, and he believes that, as a Church, "we must learn from our history or repeat it. We honor our heritage as we appreciate it and build upon it."

TRANSMITTER OF THE HERITAGE

It was this aspect of Roy's interest in the Wesleyan movement here that Bishop Earl G. Hunt, Jr., described so eloquently when he preached, in June of 1972, at his bishop colleague's retirement.

Calling the roll of some of the great ones, beginning with

BUILDER OF BRIDGES

Francis Asbury, he said: "Proudly we add another name to this company, Roy Hunter Short, who, combining sensitive spirituality with creative churchmanship as circuit preacher, district superintendent, metropolitan pastor, editor and bishop, has served well the far-flung Methodism he so dearly loves."

Then he spoke on four elements of that heritage and he outlined what Roy has been doing to pass it along, enriched by his own thinking and praying and living.

He went to Roy's little book *Spiritual Revival in Our Day* for wise directions on the lostness of humanity and the impotence of humanism, and to his *Evangelism Through the Local Church* for some suggestions that would build conviction in the Christian church.

Perception is another element in the Wesleyan heritage, and Bishop Hunt said:

"The years of his episcopacy have been a period filled with critical and turbulent issues: war, race, theological transition, the separation of church and state, ecumenism, the moral revolution, struggles for power within the Church and so on. Scores of times his brilliant and insightful analyses of the problems related to such crises as presented to the Council of Bishops in carefully prepared papers have enabled the chief pastors of the Church to understand such issues accurately and to deal with them constructively. I have often said that I never knew a person who could look farther down the road of the future and perceive with more prophetic sureness what might be expected to occur than Roy Short. To a casual observer there is often an aura of mystery about his crystal ball; but to those who know him best it is quite clear that massive study and thought, disciplined and organized by an unusually fine mind, explain his startling proficiency as a seer of things to come."

HONORING THE METHODIST HERITAGE

THE PREACHER AS MESSENGER

"Message is the communication of the great doctrine of religion clearly, vividly, fervently and effectively," said Bishop Hunt, indicating that the message is the third quality of our heritage. He named Phillips Brooks, Robert Murray McCheyne, Frederick W. Robertson, George Whitefield, Otto Dibelius, Sam Shoemaker and Roy Hunter Short.

"In a deeply satisfying way, Bishop Short has illustrated for me the haunting power of the Christian message as it is offered through preaching. There is always the danger that administrative responsibility will produce an erosion of pulpit creativity, and surely a certain amount of this is inevitable for all who have been called into connectional obligations for the Church. But I have never felt that it affected Bishop Short as much as others.

"I have never heard him preach poorly, or undertake to bring a message which did not lay a strong hold upon my own soul. The lyrical quality of his own spirit often breaks through his preaching. Occasionally he closes a message by moving into the melody of some great hymn, and this lovely practice beautifully suggests the fact that in his own heart and life theology has become doxology.[4]

"The fourth approach to our heritage is something that goes beyond the others—conviction, perception and message—and it is witness. It involves the other three and speaks primarily of the believer as a human being, a warmly compassionate person for whom the Lord Jesus Christ died."

Again, Bishop Hunt went back into history to name some leaders with whom he associates Roy Short. He mentioned the Wesleys, Francis Asbury, Peter Cartwright, Matthew Simpson, Francis J. McConnell, and John R. Mott. He had no hesitancy in putting Roy Short among them, explaining, "This may be an appropriate time to insist again upon the primacy of New Testament goodness among all of us who bear the gospel's message." He added:

"Pietism has been associated with piety and moralism with moral sensitivity—and the latter has been abandoned with the former! Cleanness of thinking, speaking and living is in many quarters no longer regarded as an unmistakable hallmark of Christian faith. But religion can never get away from the simple, devastating fact that its experience has to make a qualitative difference in a person's life and relationships. One cannot remember the teachings of Augustine, Anselm, Calvin or Wesley, much less the troublesome New Testament witness to the personal purity and devotional discipline of Jesus, without realizing that the severing of personal piety from theological reflection—indeed, from Christian discipleship—is, put mildly, a peculiar development."[5]

The description of witnessing, as exemplified by Roy Short (still "my own bishop," Bishop Hunt insisted) continued with tributes to his preaching and living: "Behind this kind of preaching is a life: a life made lean by the discipline of austerity, a life wrenched away from the soft lap of luxury and set on its pilgrim way with a ruthless solitariness of purpose, a life that has been crucified with Christ and now knows him in the full and blazing power of the Resurrection."

Bishop Hunt sums up: "As we have examined four aspects of our Wesleyan heritage it has been easy to recognize once more that institutions, even the Christian Church, are usually the lengthened shadows of individuals. So our speaking of these matters in terms of the distinguished ministry of Bishop Short has been highly appropriate."

COLLECTING MEMORIES

Roy has never put a high value on honors and awards, except as they are associated with precious memories

HONORING THE METHODIST HERITAGE

of persons, places and experiences. He has seven honorary degrees, with their citations, and numerous awards, including two Kentucky colonelcies, one presented by Governor Lawrence Wetherbee in 1951 and the other by Governor Edward Breathitt in 1967. His home church, Marcus Lindsey, has a memorial stained glass window for him. St. George's Church in Philadelphia, one of the two oldest Methodist churches in the United States, gave him its coveted award, and there have been numerous other recognitions at home and abroad.

The two that he values most came from within the boundaries of the Southeastern Jurisdiction. The citation given by Emory and Henry College came on the occasion when, in 1972, he was made a doctor of canon law. It recites some of his achievements and says:

"Perhaps the first of Bishop Roy Short's significant gifts to his Church has been his own life and the sure and sensitive faith it has reflected. Consciousness of the central verities in the Wesleyan tradition, concern that pure evangelism shall permeate the Church, eagerness to maintain the spiritual glow that comes from Christian experience and to spread its incandescence everywhere—these characteristics of his own great soul speak eloquently through his sermons, his books and his administration."

In the other honor, he joins with a company of colleague bishops in Bishops Hall at Emory University, at Atlanta. He says:

"In the parlor they have named for me there is a portrait given by the Tennessee Conference in 1960. I am eternally grateful to God for the privilege of ministering in his name with his people."

NOTES—SHORT AND LONG

1. In 1918 Bishop William Oldham wrote a biography of Bishop James M. Thoburn under the title: *Thoburn, Called of God*. Bishop Thoburn lived until 1922. The list of Episcopal biographies by other bishops follows: Bishop McConnell wrote of Bishop Andrews, Bishop Grose wrote of Bishop James W. Bashford, Bishop Capers wrote of Bishop William M. Wightman, Bishop DuBose wrote of Bishop Joshua Soule, Bishop Candler wrote of Bishop Charles B. Galloway, Bishop D. W. Clark wrote of Bishop Elijah Hedding, Bishop Bristol wrote of Bishop Charles C. McCabe, Bishop Charles B. Galloway wrote of Bishop Linus W. Parker, Bishop Hoss wrote of Bishop William McKendree, Bishop David Moore wrote of Bishop John M. Waldren and Bishop Badley wrote of Bishop Francis Warne and also of Bishop J. R. Chitambar, of India.

2. Bishop Frederick D. Leete's collection of badges, of bishops photographs, programs and other memorabilia, is unsurpassed. For a time this collection was housed in Broadway Church, Indianapolis, now lodged at Perkins School of Theology.

3. Bishop John Seybert's one-horse wagon is an illustration. He loaded it with books (some 20,000 of them) in German at the publishing house in New Berlin, Pa., and delivered them to preachers in Ohio. The wagon may be seen in a collection of Evangelical United Brethren treasures at Dayton.

4. Since theology is the study and knowledge of God and doxology is the praise of God, "From Theology to Doxology and Back," might be a suitable title for a book on Roy Short's theology.

5. Bishop Hunt comments that Nietzsche, often quoted in other connections, was once heard to shout: "These Christians must show me that they are redeemed before I will believe in their Redeemer!"

24
"I HAVE BEEN YOUNG . . . NOW I AM OLD"

Bishop G. Bromley Oxnam is the only recent bishop on record who made it clear that he was glad to retire. Shaking with a nervous disorder, he said with a grin, "I'll be content to give it up." Bishop Charles Wesley Flint, like many another, remained on the effective list when he scarcely could stand on his feet. After 24 years in the active episcopacy, Roy confesses some weariness, but he looks for things to do—and he has never taken up fishing or golf. He quotes the psalmist: "I have been young, and now I am old; yet I have not seen the righteous forsaken" (Psalm 37:25).

Roy remembers all the boys Sunday school classes he taught and how he cherished the idea, "Start a boy on the right road, and even in old age he will not leave it."

His own reverence for older persons was born in him. Time and time again in his teaching and preaching he went back to his experiences in the family circle. When he became a district superintendent and later a bishop, he tried to help young preachers. "You haven't helped me much in my career," was, in his opinion, the most severe criticism he could imagine, whether or not it was deserved. His years with The Upper Room gave him a chance to speak with youth in 48 colleges and seminaries, though he was never a seminary teacher.

During the vagaries of the "Terrible Sixties" he tried to

remember the lines of Dickens in *A Tale of Two Cities:* "It was the best of times, it was the worst of times, . . . it was the spring of hope, it was the winter of despair. . . ." In that spirit he tried to puzzle his way through the rebellion that centered around youth in Dallas in 1968, and St. Louis in 1970, as well as the World Methodist Council in Denver in 1971.

He welcomed the younger faces he saw coming into the policy-making bodies of the Church, though, to be honest about it, bearded faces on young men were a little hard for him to take. He consecrated committed youth whenever he could discover them. He thought that Richard Chevenix-Trench might be speaking for more than his own generation of youth when he said: "The newer generation is morally braver, more truthful, more serious, intelligent and frank." At the same time, Roy observes that, unhappily on occasion, disgruntled older persons encouraged honestly disillusioned youth to do things more shocking than they would normally do.

When Roy found the going hard, he remembered the many people who helped him work through his own problems and he thought of the account Jesus had of the man at the pool of Bethesda. When the waters were stirred up and had their healing powers, the crowd rushed down to the water's edge, but only the first person stepping in received healing. An old man, ill for thirty-eight years, said sadly to Jesus, "Sir, I have no man, when the water is troubled, to put me into the pool" (John 5:7). Roy's commentary: "But I have always had people to help me." Looking back to his youth and younger ministry, he recalls a multitude of such persons, most of them humble, from many different walks of life.[1]

A PARADE OF PERSONS

In reflective moments Roy finds himself reminded of a parade of personalities that, in the 60 years of his minis-

"I HAVE BEEN YOUNG . . . NOW I AM OLD"

try, have passed across the stage and captured the attention of the Church—and the whole world for that matter. To name a few, there were these theologians: Emil Brunner, Karl Barth, Rudolf Bultmann, Paul Tillich, Reinhold Niebuhr, Dietrich Bonhoeffer, John C. Bennett, Walter Horton, Henry P. Van Dusen and Harvey Cox. Each of these had his day, and then the Christian world waited for the appearance of yet another star in the theological firmament.

"Then there were the preachers who gained national and international attention, particularly as the radio and television age came on: Harry Emerson Fosdick, Stanley Jones, Billy Graham, Ralph Sockman, and Archbishop Fulton Sheen, who died only a few days before this was written.

"Among the Church leaders were such tall figures as Francis Cardinal Spellman, Rufus Jones, Elton Trueblood, John R. Mott, W. A. Visser t' Hooft and D. T. Niles.

"Most of them are gone now, but they are being followed by others who are now taking their own place in the endless line of splendor."

A SERIES OF CRISES

"I don't know how, precisely, to draw a graph of the Church, with its upswings and downward trends since I have known it, but I am sure that the general curve moves upwards toward the True Church that is yet to be.

"Yes, there have been crises during the sixties in which I have seen the Church greatly threatened: the controversy over evolution, the Fundamentalist-Modernist arguments, the Social Gospel versus Personal Gospel dispute, the volcanic disturbance over higher criticism, the appearance of the death-of-God 'theologians' and the turmoil that became so general. I have lived through them all, and I have discovered that the Church can live with Crisis, however difficult it may seem to be at the moment."

A SUCCESSION OF HOPES

"Paul used the expression, 'when hope seems hopeless,' and there have been times when this state of mind and heart described the times in which we have lived, yet I have found several good reasons for hoping beyond hope in the Christian way.

"There is the hope to be found in the missionary outreach of the Church, as represented 50 years ago, in the slogan, 'The Evangelization of the World in This Generation.' The world did not see its achievement in the time frame we once had in mind, but nevertheless great gains on every continent on earth and on the islands of the seas. The great missionary councils preceding the Second World War offered further hope for missions. Then in the early thirties came the stimulating study, 'Rethinking Missions,' with its fresh appraisal of missionary goals and methods.

"Most important of all, so far as the missionary movement is concerned, during the years of my own ministry, has been the growth of the indigenous church, and the development of national leadership that has proved itself able, vigorous and fully dedicated. In my own beginning ministry the Church was still planting the gospel in what we then called 'the mission field.' Today we are witnessing the harvest of that planting.

"Another hope was represented by the Social Gospel, so strongly advocated in the days of my beginning ministry and so shattered by the depression and the war.

"The hope of world peace was like a shining star in the twenties and early thirties. The peace about which we dreamed is still an elusive hope, but it remains a hope. The

"I HAVE BEEN YOUNG . . . NOW I AM OLD"

Bishops' Crusade for Peace in the forties represented a genuine contribution, and the Council of Bishops is concerned to emphasize 'Peace and the Self-development of Peoples,' with particular stress upon the things that make for peace.

"I see another hope for the Church in its determination to purify itself, with God's help, through self-criticism and self-discipline. I take courage in the impact of the Church on government. It must be acknowledged that a host of government organizations designed to minister to human need had their inception in the consciences of church people who saw that social problems of tremendous magnitude cannot be cured by band-aid philanthropy.

"There is lasting hope in the fascination that great minds and warm hearts find in the creative ideas—sometimes starburst clusters of them—that come in succession. I think of such things as the stewardship of all of life, new methods of constructive counseling, the small group emphasis and the establishment of retreat centers.

"Another source of hope is the emphasis on the cooperation between churches as expressed in community, state, national, regional and world councils, (with their numerous activities); in new Roman Catholic-Protestant relationships; and in continuing conversation on church union. All these matters, however, are not without their difficulties and complications. Furthermore, I realize now, as I have not always known, that there are competing parties within every religious movement, and that Christians in the developing countries often have sects and cults for which Western Christians have no counterpart.[2]

"Louise and I are committed to traveling the itinerant road until the end, doing whatever good we can, until the fever of life is over, and our work is done, and we find at last the rest which 'remaineth . . . to the people of God.' "

NOTES—SHORT AND LONG

1. In "Memories of Childhood and Youth" the saintly doctor and musician, Albert Schweitzer wrote similarly: "One thing stirs me when I look back at my youthful days—the fact that so many people gave me something or were something to me—without knowing it."

2. Among the Chinese on Taiwan, for example, the real differences were not between Methodists and Presbyterians, Lutherans and Seventh Day Adventists, but between such "mainline denominations" and the larger independent groups like the Little Flock, the True Jesus Church, the True Jesus Family Church and others for which there are no Western counterparts.